# JERRY WOLMAN:

# THE WORLD'S RICHEST MAN

As told to
Joseph Bockol
& Richard Bockol

Heritage Special Edition
**American Literary Press**
*Arnold, Maryland*

# JERRY WOLMAN: THE WORLD'S RICHEST MAN

Library of Congress
Cataloging-in-Publication Data
ISBN-13: 978-1-934696-45-3

Collector's Edition ISBN-13: 978-1-934696-46-0

cover image of football field © Suprijono Suharjoto | Dreamstime.com
cover image of eagle © Miao | Dreamstime.com

Published by

Heritage Special Edition
American Literary Press

1290 Bay Dale Drive, Suite 297
Arnold, Maryland 21012

Manufactured in the United States

*With most appreciated help from:*
Anne Bockol, Claire Buete, Leo Carlin, Lou Diamond,
Doug Doan, Gaeton Fonzi, Jim Gallagher, Robert Hirsch, Esq.,
Joe King, Sam Matta, Bob Melnick, Josephine Putnam,
Wilma Robel, Ed Sabol, Steve Sabol, Jerry Schiff,
Howard Steinhardt, Charles Tatelbaum, Esq. and Bruce Wolman

*Dedicated to:*
Anne, Bobbie, Helene, Lenny, Alan, Michelle, Adam,
Robyn, Derek, Julie, Jared, Brian, Danny, Andie,
Michael, Susan, David, Danny, Val and Sandy

# PROLOGUE

You can't say that someone didn't warn wealthy building tycoon and professional sports owner Jerry Wolman of impending monetary disaster. Not that he would have, nor did he, heed the ominous foreboding.

In early 1965, he attended a cocktail and dinner party in Los Angeles given by his sister Sandy. She had invited, among other Hollywood luminaries, the famous comedian Red Buttons and his spouse. Button's wife was a spiritual South American woman who prided herself in being able to tell one's fortune with the precision of an oracle. She began, after drinking a few Pisco Sours, to read the seemingly most fortunate palms of almost half a dozen guests to everyone's glee. The sixth was Sandy, the hostess herself. Button's wife turned semi-serious, and advised Sandy that she would "soon be divorced, but had a brighter future." Wolman was stunned by the remarks because he knew at the time that Sandy was no longer in love with her then husband. In order to deflect the modified mood created by the teller's words, Sandy turned to her brother Jerry whose levity she was counting on to break the somber spell that had just been cast. "Let her read your palm, Jerry. Go next."

Wolman was the lucky seventh, and he approached the South American as if she were Carmen Miranda balancing too much fruit on her headdress. Nevertheless, with a wink to all those watching, and hoping to engender a laugh, he said, "I'm not Sandy's husband."

After a brief examination, Red Button's wife instantly turned crimson, then ashen. She simply refused to speak after having

1

*lifted his outstretched palm, except to say, "No...No, I cannot say any more." She looked him in the eyes and repeated her adamant reluctance, rejecting his palm in no uncertain terms. Wolman's smile disappeared. He was ninety-nine percent certain she had no idea who he was, and therefore her concern seemed troubling, especially in light of the previous revelation that she'd bull's-eyed regarding his sister.*

*Wolman asked her as jovially as he could not to hesitate. He never believed in fortune-telling as anything other than hocus pocus to begin with. "Go ahead; it's not a problem," he insisted with bravado. Having amassed nothing but success after success in his mind and pocket, and having become one of the world's richest men, he was all but invincible. Wolman's empire was huge, glamorous and growing. "What could she possibly say to dent my armor?" he thought. "Nothing bad can happen."*

*She finally spoke slowly and bluntly. "You are going to go broke. You're going to lose everything you have. But on the good side of things," she emphasized, "you're then gonna come back bigger and stronger than ever." Wolman just glared and would not give up his smile. He was convinced then that he must pay no attention to so pessimistic a prognosis. And he didn't.*

*Jerry Wolman will now readily admit that whether the South American woman was right or wrong, he does not know. He did go broke and he did lose everything. However, the only claim he will add to that uncomfortable confirmation, "She's kept me believing all these years that I'm going to come back bigger and stronger than ever!"*

*On a whim, about forty years later, Wolman did ask his remarried sister Sandy to contact Red Button's wife, to request that the aging fortune-teller answer just one question:*

*"WHEN?"*

# Christmas Eve, 1967

A fierce Northeastern cold filled the December night in Philadelphia as if the city were a meat locker. Jerry Wolman had been hung on a hook, spiraling in an unraveling downturn. His knuckles nearly froze to the trunk of his car as he tried his keys to unlock and pry it open. He had many problems; literally in the tens of millions. His empire had all but collapsed and all he had was almost gone. But at Christmas, there were still those less fortunate he had to reach that night. Making certain the trunk was empty to handle the toys he was about to buy, he looked upward for a time at signs of stars, and backwards in time to his mother Sadie's advice. She had requested of her young cherub son that if he ever got "lucky," he should "always be good to other people." He thought of his mother as saintly, and claimed she had already lived nine lives: all of them her children. Wolman recalled vividly that she was as selfless as any human on earth.

Thinking back to Shenandoah, when he was no more than a tireless tyke, young Wolman endeavored to make his own luck; requiring himself to adhere to his mother's plea. Even before he was a teen, at Christmas and Chanukah each year, he put together baskets of vegetables and fruits from his father's warehouse, for slightly less flush families. Some of the produce was not pristine enough to sell, but surely to him looked adequate enough to gift. He'd go to the coal mines and chip away black chunks to put into bags to sell for 25 cents apiece. Then he'd buy fresh turkeys with the money to add to the baskets. Wolman continued this childhood practice for almost

3

a decade in his town, being especially kind to anyone who'd been good to him and his family. His mother beamed as he left home to make the deliveries, stars twinkling in her eyes.

Years later in 1963, after he'd bought the Philadelphia Eagles and had come to town as a multi-millionaire, he surreptitiously and anonymously renewed his mother's wishes in the city of Brotherly Love. He and his best, longest and most rotund friend from Shenandoah, Johnny Robel (who was now the Eagles' newest and highest paid equipment manager in the league), ventured out all night on every Christmas Eve to buy and package, in pompous wrappings with twirling ribbons, toys for children in Philadelphia's hospitals. They delivered games and dolls and colorful presents, never identifying themselves, disguised in costume; often avoiding hospital staff and, almost as often, never even waking or disturbing the sick kids from their needed sleep. Many of the children in these wards had no one else. The mere thought of hundreds of youngsters awakening to beds and cots brimming with brilliantly colored prizes in bows made Wolman embrace his geometrically growing luck. He annually reconnected with Sadie's suggestion through the wondrous expressions on the faces of the children. For Jerry Wolman, there was no greater joy.

On Christmas Eve 1967, however, Jerry Wolman was unshaven and perilously close to penniless. The forty-year-old tycoon, who had seen his unfettered upswing in the pages of *Time* magazine as the success of the century, was now drowning in Time's first pages on November 24th, 1967. The article was titled, "Business: in Deep Water." It graphically described Wolman's announcement that he'd managed to lose $15,500,000 "recently," and that he needed over $7,000,000 "right now" just to survive. His creditors numbered in the hundreds, and he had liabilities nearing an unfathomable $90,000,000. Time reported that Wolman's insurance obligations and back taxes remained unpaid totaling a half million dollars. His bank accounts were severely overdrawn. Turkeys seemed out of place this holiday season, 1967. Once heralded as the "Boy Wonder" for his Midas touch, there was simply no reason for a man in his position to be thankful.

As pundits predicted, on December 13th, 1967, Wolman filed

a Bankruptcy Petition under Chapter XI in the District Court of Maryland. The weight of his woes was unrelenting. Wolman remembers to this day the Bankruptcy Court Clerk's filing number for his case: "13072." He'd lost all control of everything. Nearly every cent of the money that he'd worked for was gone; pursued by the heated hands of committees of creditors and judgmental judges. Not only had he lost; he *was* lost.

Nevertheless, Wolman called Robel the day before Christmas Eve that year to get a driver so they could get going as always. They packed the car's trunk with so many boxes of toys that Rudolph the Red-Nosed Reindeer's nose was green with envy. Through children's cancer wards and packed hospital units, the pair pranced quietly and gingerly. If a youngster awakened, they mimed and mimicked the playfulness of real Santas. All of their eyes, including the men's, were glistening and glad. Only once were the gifts momentarily halted. A guard was unsure of Wolman's and Robel's intentions, well outside of visiting hours. The guard cautiously approached the pair and asked the least imposing, Wolman, what he thought he was doing, and who he was. "The name is NAMLOW," replied Wolman in reverse, so as to remain discrete and impossible to trace. The guard's face tightened and peered at Namlow. There occurred a glimmer of recognition. The inquisitor smiled as graciously as the children had at the Mad-Hattered man with gifts. "Thanks," the guard hushed his response, and looked to Robel, "thank you."

When all was unsaid and done, the two returned to the car and simply cried behind its frozen windows. Robel, who resembled a 246 pound bamboo-gnashing pink panda, was known to drive Wolman to drink. And on that night, they drank plenty.

On December 27th, 1967, *Philadelphia Daily News* sports columnist Bill Shefski got wind of the duo's long night (possibly from the inquisitive hospital guard). A tough writer who worked Wolman over dependably, and a reporter whose heart had been hardened by many sports figures in the area, became heartened by the pre-Christmas Eve's kindnesses. His article's headline, delivered to press that afternoon in the "Four Star" edition blared "The Insolvent Santa." It followed with this poem:

"Twas two nights before Christmas
And all through the land,
Not a rich man was stirring-
Except Jerry Wolman
The stockings were hung at some hospitals
with care,
With no hopes of St. Nicholas ever
arriving there.
While affluent gentlemen snuggled up in their beds,
Insolvent Santa fulfilled the dream
in poor children's heads."

Shefski concluded, "Not many of the people after Jerry Wolman's scalp will be impressed with this story either. But they do not matter. All that matters is that Jerry Wolman prevented some little people, whose health had abandoned them from thinking that Santa had abandoned them too."

# Shenandoah, Pennsylvania

In the last half of the 1930's, "Shendo" as the locals often compressed its name, was a densely populated small village of twenty-five thousand tough, hard-working and honest-to-the-bone inhabitants. Houses had been built so close to each other that you could whisper your neighbor "good-night" if both had windows open at bedtime.

The clutter of nearly one hundred and fifty bars or social clubs, and over forty churches, ironically allowed for the coexistence of raucousness and religion. However, there was little doubt about which favorable preferences Shenandoah elected officials provided their constituents: A town Ordinance set forth that no bar could be established or opened within one block of a church. So, whenever and/or wherever a taproom was contemplated, the politicians instantly required that the church move at least a block away.

Often described as "the only Wild West town in the East," Shenandoah's population endured a rough-and-tumble existence. Playing cards and betting on the "numbers" at paltry "pools," and drinking endless shots and beers in dimly lit canteens after work, caused all men to be coarsely reddened and poker-faced. Needless to say, a street corner fight was as commonplace as a lamp post. With their miners' arms and chests, a stare down from the average Shenandoan would cause even the great John Wayne to gulp.

Nevertheless, it was a time and place where no one locked his or her doors. In fact, keys to any home were left openly dangling on a string in front of each respective front porch door. Frankly, there was little time to fear or be suspicious of anyone. Too much energy had to be spent raising a family and earning a living: too much back-breaking work to do, and carousing to accomplish, of which certainly no one was afraid or distrustful.

On the very afternoon before Valentine's Day in 1927, Jerry Wolman was born via mid-wife (and mother Sadie) in Shenandoah into one of its approximately one hundred Jewish families. He entered this life screaming with energy before the mid-wife even attempted a slap. The infant was born in a third floor apartment as the fourth of what was to be a family of nine children. His alleged birth certificate reads "Baby Wolman," but not without a bit of mystery. The arrival of the certificate occurred later, so he's never been certain which of the Baby Wolman's to whom it refers. Therefore, he could be a few surprised years older or younger than he surmises. The family of eleven lived in a three bedroom apartment situated directly above "Schoor's" grocery store. The rising warmth from the oven of his mother's kosher kitchen arrived from directly below the family bedrooms.

Pennsylvania's industrial growth in the early 20th century required an immense need for laborers. Immigration from Wales supplied the first wave of strong men, especially those with experience in Welsh coal mining. Families from Ireland, Poland, Russia and Italy followed anthracite suit. The ethnic aromas of potatoes and cabbage, baked Kielbasa, crusted Feta cheese, sizzling Cheese Blintzes and fresh baked fruit pies permeated Shenandoah's air. It seemed an ideal place to open a food or produce business. The coal miners' appetites and thirsts were legendary. They were hell bent on nourishing and alleviating a long sooty day's growing hunger and darkened underground sobriety.

In 1907 Wolman's grandparents on his father's side came from Poland to the United States, and directly to Ellis Island. One of the grandfather's cousins who had preceded him, and was now residing in Mt. Carmel, Pennsylvania, mentioned the then booming mining industry in nearby Shenandoah. The cousin suggested the establishment of a grocery store there. And so, the Wolman family became food entrepreneurs among numerous nationalities and religions.

Wolman's father, the toughest of his family's seven children, stayed within the family tradition and continued a produce supplier's wholesale "warehouse." Hot-tempered as his own mother, who many said clearly resembled Mussolini in stature, girth and temperament, Solly would take a punch at you at the least provocation. And God forbid if someone stole even a nickel's worth of smelts from the stands outside his store, he'd chase the culprit for blocks until he caught and thrashed him to an orange pulp.

*****

At five years old, before commencing school, young Jerry was awakened by his father at sunrise, and told succinctly and gruffly, "It's time to go to work." Half asleep, he was led by Mr. Wolman to the warehouse cellar with instructions to wash tomatoes, trim celery and clean the produce for that day's sales. Except for Shabbat, this daily couple of hour's work continued throughout the year and did not stop although Jerry had turned six and was now starting his first grade schooling. Once it began, he was given only a few minutes to run home from work, wash up, and race to school. His father paid Jerry 15 cents a week of which he gave 10 cents to his mother for room and board.

On his eighth birthday, Jerry obtained his first "outside job" plucking salted blood-drained chickens at Bernie Schoor's Kosher Butcher Shop down the street. Mr. Schoor offered Jerry 15 cents per naked chicken. Jerry grabbed at the opportunity, leaving his father livid. But the job didn't last a day. Realizing that eliminating the underlying pin-feathers from only one bird could last a perfectionist like him a week, he meekly returned to his father as a prodigal, sullen, smelly and itching son. Not a word was said between them, as their former routine was re-established instantly. Year after year, the young boy was given more tasks, and was now working before and after school. By age ten, in his spare time, and to obtain ice cream money, the beleaguered youngster traipsed the streets with a cart of fruits to sell from house to house. A large yellow lemon in his mouth, he'd squeeze and remove it only to pucker for what seemed like a kiss as a housewife opened her door. The housewives were embarrassed and delighted at the child-salesman's embellishment, and laughingly bought more lemons than they needed for that evening's pot of tea.

In fifth grade, Jerry's teacher, Miss Lovina Sampsel, sensed how hard he was working from his drawn demeanor and tired eyes, and soon learned of his situation. Feeling the same great empathy for children that enlivened her teaching for the previous thirty years, the hefty fifty year-old spinster kindly asked the tired waif to go to the back of the room and rest his head on the desk to get some sleep, while the other students sat at attention behind their desks learning. When classes ended, she gently poked and awakened him. Miss Sampsel told him what had already been taught that day and used her unpaid overtime every afternoon to keep Jerry's mind up to date. The gray-haired mentor soon took a special guardian angel's interest in Jerry and began building his self-confidence. She noted his brilliance with numbers and his energy (when refreshed) to learn and retain facts as if with a photographic memory. She offered him advice and made him believe he could do anything he put his mind to. She became his third parent. From the time Wolman was twenty-five, and mindful of his own first tastes of success, he went out of his way to find Miss Sampsel, and send her bouquets of flowers on Mother's Day each and every year for decades until her death.

# Flying, Robel And Football

On the more colorful side of Jerry Wolman's childhood, from his earliest memories there were reveries of doing magical things. At age five, despite the relentless work ethic hammered into his psyche, his imagination had begun to grow in leaps and bounds. In fact, he began to believe and was certain he could fly. One afternoon, having adorned his slim muscular body with a red cape tied soundly around his neck, the boy pranced to one of the third floor bedrooms. Not telling a soul, he opened its window facing the rear yard. Looking down, he could see the roof of the first floor porch which extended outward below him for about ten feet. Also in view was the cement patio surrounding the base of the porch three floors below. Jerry's final flight plan was to soar like an eagle over the porch and then gracefully glide on his belly, sliding along the slippery-smooth surface of ground-level concrete. His aerial confidence was so strong he suddenly thought that the cape was unnecessary. But why take chances? Jumping with a swan dive worthy of Johnny Weissmuller, he posed his spread arms as if Tarzan in an attempt to save Jane. Grinning, and bearing the ascending air through his nostrils, he closed his eyes in weightless joy and flew effortlessly.

The youngster remembered little else other than being rushed to the hospital with a ripped open jaw and a tearful mother close and holding him. His chin, now deeply scarred and bloody, had clipped a nail on the edge of the porch's roof, ripping open a four inch gash in his skin. But alas, there was not another scratch or bruise on his body anywhere. The landing must have been patio-perfect; the cement runway no more hardened than a silky pillow. In later life, taking similarly concocted daring leaps in business became habitual. One thing was evident: from the time he was a young child, neither the natural laws of gravity nor the skies would be his limit. Even at such an early age, he genuinely thrived on and believed that the unthinkable deserved consideration and that the impossible was attainable.

These same principles became the nascent core of his business endeavors. He perceived early on that buying and selling required promises on both sides. His father's meticulous handling of produce, pushing himself and his son through hours of preparation and sales, constrained them to sell well and buy prudently. It was also ingrained in his mind that when buying, to pay as quickly as you would have wished to have been paid yourself. Religion and cash-on-hand often co-mingled problems. On High Holy Days, for instance, the orthodox fasting Wolman family had turned off all lights (including the one in the refrigerator) throughout their home and store, and all were forbidden to use water for cleaning and brushing teeth. Jerry was always at synagogue, starving, squeezed between his devout father and grandfather. For hours upon long restless hours, squinting and shuddering, he endured the rancid smell and the painful odor of his two elders' breath. To make matters worse, they seemingly took turns smacking his fingers or pinching his thigh for not paying full attention to the Hebrew phrases.

When services ended, Jerry secretly ran as fast as he could to the Center Street movie house. Jerry's acceleration was completely unrelated to the feature film, but instead for the welcome smells of popcorn and peace at hand. Management at the theater allowed Jews credit for the day since the orthodox were not allowed to carry money. Joe Dalton, The Strand movie house manager on Main Street saw plenty of Jewish children escaping to the movies on the Jewish holy days, but only Jerry returned the following day to make payment. Owing money for this business-child was entirely out of the question. Making a promise required that it be instantly kept.

*****

12

The most momentous occasion of his childhood, including the domains of dutiful work patterns, dreamy aspirations and rigid religious observances, was Jerry's unharmonious musical meeting of his lifelong friend, Johnny Robel. The chance event happened in fifth grade at Jefferson Elementary School while the two were attempting to select instruments for the school's youth-filled marching band. Both reached for and simultaneously grabbed the one and only trombone.

"I think I have it," Robel growled with sharpness familiar to street-wise Wolman as a threat to let go. Senselessly, and in the face of Robel's advantageous girth and height, Wolman glared upwards to counter, "I don't think you do; I think I have it." The argument that ensued was carried outside for a full-fledged fistfight and wrestling match.

Robel quickly punched Wolman to the ground, braced his knees on Wolman's shoulders and knocked him about with abandon. With no holds barred, Robel began to systematically pound the back of Wolman's wobbly head upon the asphalt under it. Johnny's huge hands grasped his opponent's head as if it were a grapefruit from which he was determined to squirt juice. Finally, in an act of sheer mercy, Robel asked the almost unconscious and incontinent Wolman, "Do you give up?"

In his pinned position, Jerry replied with all the vigor he could muster. "Get off me before I killya."

Johnny Robel was the son of one of Shenandoah's Polish legends, Jolly Jack Robel, who had composed the most famous tune to emerge from the mining town: "The Beer Barrel Polka." Johnny's musical talent had not fallen far from his father's brew. When he determined that Jerry was too dumb to keep pummeling, Johnny offered the trombone to his helpless opponent. Of course, feigning victory, Jerry insisted that he would relinquish the brass instrument because he no longer wanted it. Robel's laughter could be heard as far away as the suburbs of Scranton. They shook hands in exhaustion, and neither ever had a better friend thereafter. Johnny's trombone playing led the school band while Jerry took small satisfaction in becoming the band's first marching French horn enthusiast.

The two were inseparable in all things, but playing football together was the ultimate, as they fantasized that they were playing in the National Football League. Both were scrappy young men, mischievous and brazenly bold with body contacts. Because of their hard-nosed countenances and reputations, they were not allowed by their peers to play on the same team. Everyone grasped that only Robel could hit Wolman hard enough to stop him; and only Wolman would clip Robel at the knees, bite his leg and/or slash at Robel's Adam's apple to bring him down. The terrain upon which they battled was grassless and replete with rocks. They played with the minors of miners who never missed an opportunity to curse, fight, and cause horrendous welts on an opposing player's skin. Purple clouds of pigskin bruises were common on all sides, well beyond the composition of a kaleidoscope's "black and blue."

*****

In the late 1930's, if the Philadelphia Eagles had a home game, the pre-teen adolescent pair would hitchhike over a hundred miles to Municipal Stadium in South Philadelphia, then a few years later to Shibe Park in North Philadelphia. Each game, Jerry and Johnny waited outside the gate in the cold, only to be let in for free at the end of the first half by an unspoken Stadium rule and a sympathetic security guard. Half an Eagles game was better than none and met the only price of admission they could afford. Once inside, the electric sights and sounds from the game and crowd made the two shivering outsiders feel the heat of something truly special. Though the Eagles rarely won, they loved the team and its star players, quarterback Davey O'Brien and receiver Don Looney, and discussed every play with great animation to the delight of the driver from whom they'd hitched their way back to Shenandoah.

*****

On weekdays, by the age of fourteen, Jerry was driving his father's 10 ton truck in the evening from home to Philadelphia's Dock Street Terminal. His nighttime journey was a hundred and thirty hard miles in order to reach the Terminal's opening at 1:00 a.m. The truck had to be loaded with ten tons of produce for return to Shenandoah. In the dangerous absence of a driver's license and a union card, Jerry completed the late night sorting and lifting, often in the face of threats and a few beatings from disgruntled union members. Johnny Robel began to join Jerry on some of these trips in order to keep his friend company, to discuss their Eagles and to help with lifting the sacks of food. Robel also provided fabulous protection. There wasn't a year from the time he was fifteen that Johnny Robel didn't surpass everyone in Shenandoah (or almost anywhere else they traveled) in width, mass and strength.

Jerry'd arrive back with the loaded truck at 5:00 a.m., attempting to catch an hour or two of sleep after unloading and getting himself washed and dressed. Then, off to school.

He would leave Shenandoah behind again that same evening as before. The sleepless teenager did so without reprieve and without question for what seemed a very long, long time. He persevered up until the first month of his senior year of high school when suddenly his father suffered an unfortunate stroke. Then everything changed for the worse.

# The Shenandoah "Drop-out"

Jerry's relationship with his father was based upon an innate feeling of respect. Neither liked the other very much, just loved the other in the way that opposites attract. Jerry's father saw his son as a carefree spirit, and was not happy with a lot of things he did. Freedom from one's father is not a cherished practice of the orthodox. To the contrary, his father prescribed unquestioning obedience as the norm, and appropriate at all times. "Honor Thy Father and Thy Mother" is a Commandment. Jerry saw any extension of Moses' Tablet's terminology as servitude.

When Jerry was working in the warehouse, as an example, his father would go home to nap in the early afternoon, and return to the warehouse just before closing at 4:00 p.m. when the produce business was over. Instead of being able to go home or join Robel or others for some fun, Jerry waited as his father started moving stock around the floor. He'd order Jerry by pointing to reposition a multitude of 50 pound bags of onions twenty feet to the right or left, so that Sol Wolman could leisurely sweep the floor spotted by onion skins. He'd then command Jerry with a glance to return the bags back to their former place. Due to his ever-so-difficult disposition, "Salty Balls" was the earned nickname given to Jerry's father throughout Shenandoah.

Despite the unfairness of what seemed to be ungrateful gratuitous overtime, Jerry was torn. He admired his father's toughness and ability to raise and support a wife and nine children with no more than a third grade education, a stint in the Army as World War I began, and service in the Navy after a bout of AWOL from the Army.

He passed on to his son one important characteristic. The elder Wolman was probably as good with numbers as anyone Jerry would ever meet, taking hundreds of varied orders daily with over thirty to sixty items listed. Within seconds each and every time, he'd tell you the bottom line. Jerry inherited the same ability with real estate ventures later in life, when his mind effortlessly memorized mortgages, interest rates, valuations by square foot and principal balances due on hundreds of on-going development projects. And foremost, he listened closely when his father swore to God, nodding into his son's eyes, "You can never get hurt taking a profit."

When Sol Wolman became disabled by his stroke, he insisted that his son quit school in his senior year and take care of the family business. Jerry's older brothers were in the service, unable to aid at home, crushing Jerry's hopes of graduating with his JW Cooper High School class. His aspirations of becoming a lawyer or rabbi dashed, his future would have to await his father's hoped-for quick recovery. Jerry thought it was the right thing to do, and did so, dropping out of school one full year short of attaining a diploma with due respect to his father's wishes.

# War For Wolman And Robel

Officially taking control, all areas of the family business were now administered by Jerry. Calling the stores for products, making and taking orders, picking up and delivering produce, buying, selling and driving were suddenly all of the overwhelmed seventeen year old's sole burdens. Recovering with a newly palsied facial paralysis, Solly reviewed Jerry's weekly statements; first from his Naval Hospital bed in Philadelphia, and after a month's stay, from home. Despite being weakened, Sol's eyes and attitude for whatever his son was doing were sharper than ever. The numbers had to be positive and painstakingly exact.

*****

At the time, Shenandoah was entrenched in the upcoming election between Franklin D. Roosevelt and his Republican challenger Thomas Dewey. In this small war-time town, President Roosevelt's fourth term was all but assured. Every person was imbued with patriotism, each residence proudly displaying one-starred flags from porches and doorways signifying a son, daughter, brother, sister, husband or wife in the service of their country. FDR's speeches fired up homes as if by flaming coal stoves rather than over radio waves. The hatred for Germany and Japan was felt with such animosity that every human being in Shenandoah was flexing to fight for the USA.

Sol Wolman already had his two oldest sons fighting in the war as he returned to the warehouse in early November 1944, fully recovered but for the palsy, and needed his son Jerry at home to work. However, Jerry's burning sense of pervasive patriotic duty provided him with the courage to run away from home and enlist in the Navy; but not without the company of his best friend Johnny Robel.

Johnny grew pale listening to Jerry's scheme for both of them to become sailors in the naval forces. Jerry reiterated his plea to his soon-to-be comrade at arms, "We've got to do something to help win this war; we'll be toe to toe like always." Robel was honest with his hell-bent buddy and extremely apprehensive, growing more and more nauseous at the thought of lying to his parents, running away, and betraying his good Catholic family's bond. Johnny was happy at home and not in any way ready to leave the physical and psychological comfort of his seventeen-year-old existence. Too fearfully young for war and content to stay forever in Shenandoah, or at least until he was of age to be drafted, Johnny refused. Jerry pressed his best friend to the hilt. Pushing his index finger into Robel's chest and pounding on his own, he screamed, "What d'ya have a yellow streak on your back?" Badgering, berating and bragging of their closeness, their unity for the United States for over an hour, Jerry halted and stood at ease. Silence was solidly between them. But one thing always remained true over his lifetime...Johnny Robel was as loyal a friend anyone could have. Finally, frightened, with his head in his hands shaking "no," Johnny agreed.

In 1944, young recruits would report to enlist, and after having passed the physical, they were sent directly to boot camp; no looking back. Johnny lied about where he was going to his parents, "Hitching a ride with Jerry. Nowhere in particular, probably to Philly." Jerry made no contact before leaving. Both understood the rules of their engagement. The Navy was now to be their home for at least the next two years.

They hitched a ride to Philadelphia's Selective Service Board where they each signed on the dotted line in front of a smiling recruiting officer. Having enlisted in the Navy, they were escorted into separate rooms for their physicals before being shipped out for basic training.

In minutes, Johnny Robel had passed the routine physical. "You're in fine condition, young man," said the examining doctor matter-of-factly, "you'll be shipping out in an hour. Put your clothes back on and report for duty."

Jerry Wolman flunked his exam. "You're going nowhere Mr. Wolman. You have a heart murmur, son, and feet as flat as a blown tire." Murmur and all, thinking only of his poor best friend, Jerry's heart sank directly to his flat feet.

When Johnny Robel digested what Jerry was telling him and could fully comprehend the meaning of the news being reported to him in Wolman's anxiously paced "Walter Winchell" tones, his knees buckled. Robel's neck veins pumped and pounded as his face turned Navy blue. Jerry paced backwards in defense. As Johnny's eyes glazed over, in his grizzly guttural voice, Johnny vomited, "I'll killya."

Robel was in tears when he left, as he had no intention of going anywhere to begin with, and certainly not without Wolman. The two did not see each other face to face for years thereafter. Robel was sent by his commander to the South Pacific aboard a ship upon which he was to suffer uncontrollable chronic sea-sickness. On calmer waters, Johnny went on to win championship boxing events throughout his naval career.

# Williamsport, Pennsylvania

The enlisting officer saw Jerry's devastation, and suggested he go immediately to Williamsport, Pennsylvania to make application for the Merchant Marines. Physicals, it was advised, were not as stringent. Knowing he could not go home, he thumbed a ride to Williamsport before nightfall. Disheveled but determined, Jerry appeared the next morning at the Williamsport Technical Institute. Before he made formal application for induction, he was told by a professor of the extreme demand and need for radio officers. But that required a recruit to pass an open course before becoming such a specialist. Jerry immediately enrolled as a radio officer cadet-in-training. In the dead of a bitter winter, the course's learning curve was dense and difficult. His mental stamina was never more tested. When Christmas arrived, the ground was wet and white. All of the cadets had gone home for a short holiday; all but Jerry. On Christmas night in 1944, the seventeen-year-old runaway had no one to be with and nowhere to go. He walked and ruminated for hours in utter loneliness. Rumors that his father was likely on his trail were inflicting his brain with guilt and anticipated brutal retribution.

Jerry stumbled into an ice cream parlor whose windows were a haze of frost, tracking in cumulus clouds of snow along the checkered floor. The juke box blared The Andrews Sisters singing their hit song, "Don't Fence Me In." Jerry could not help admonishing himself under his misting breath. What a mistake he had seemingly made, breaking down his own fences. Listening to the melody and lyrics, sadness overcame him. Thoughts of home, his family and Robel

21

brought streams of tears melting the chill from his cheeks. Suddenly, an angel appeared. An attentive young waitress noticed the six-foot teen sobbing, and struck up a conversation. Not even realizing his youth, she took pity on Jerry and insisted he spend Christmas dinner with her family. She explained that she was just twenty-three, new on the job, and had never seen a *man* cry that hard. Jerry was so grateful for the lovely brunette's invitation, he would not correct her regarding his age.

After her shift, he was escorted to her home which had been decorated with Christmas lights blinking red and green and with intermittent spiraling candy canes. She unlocked a large front door and led him to the family's dining room. The long table was set for only three. A sprig of mistletoe hung from the doorframe between the kitchen and dining room. She led him below it, turned out the lights and seductively whispered, "My parents are at Evening Mass." Jerry solemnly closed his eyes and prayed. His prayers were answered after a rustle of partial mutual disrobing.

The accommodating waitress' parents soon arrived in the driveway earlier than expected, and the sound and lights of their car caused quite an instantaneous panic between the youthful strangers. Once inside, neither parent guessed at a thing, and accepted the introduction of the young cadet as a stroke of their kind virginal daughter's generous Christmas spirit. Nor did either parent observe Jerry's obvious attempt to block the fruit bowl centerpiece on the table from view. He quickly maneuvered his hand toward the bowl from behind his back, retrieving a pair of red panties enmeshed in its holiday wreath. The undergarment quickly disappeared into Jerry's pocket.

The turkey dinner with real cranberry sauce and chestnut-sausage mushroom stuffing was bountiful. Jerry watched closely and reverently as the family exchanged gifts with love and genuine emotions of graciousness. He knew at that moment the holiday meal had saved his life from depressing despair. He noted the kindness that should always occur between parents and their children. The contrast with his father's strict and senseless discord was making his spine contract. Jerry left her house at 2:00 a.m. with lifted spirits and skipped back to his dorm in the melting snow. To this day, if Jerry

Wolman hears The Andrews Sisters singing in harmony, his eyes fill with reminiscent tears.

*****

Jerry immersed himself in his studies at the Institute. He had arranged a call home to speak briefly with his mother and assured her he was safe. She confided that his father had found out where he was, and was coming within a week to take him home forcefully. After hanging up the telephone, he ran to his instructor's room at school and informed Professor Harrington that he was ready to take the test for admission, there and then, even though months of lessons remained. Having boned up in the last few days, Jerry felt confident. The professor reluctantly agreed and sent him to the Examining Board in Philadelphia for the exam. Extraordinary luck connived to have Jerry pass, but for the important portion requiring expertise in deciphering Morse code. He was told the test would be re-given in thirty days. With his father's footsteps almost audible, he begged for an immediate re-test on Morse code. The examiner directed Jerry to take an overnight course on Market Street at a school that stayed open all night just for such occasions.

Jerry trained with dots and dashes from mid-night 'til 8:00 a.m. He walked the streets and practiced by translating every sign he saw into Morse code. The test was administered at 9:00 and Jerry was proclaimed as having passed. Later learning of how desperate the Merchant Marines were for radio officers, Jerry never was sure if he actually passed by his own merits. Nonetheless, he was sworn in at 10:00, fitted for a uniform and given a bus ticket by 11:00. He reported to Newport News, Virginia that afternoon to present himself on a large troop carrier named "The William R. Lewis." That same day, Jerry and William sailed to Liverpool with hundreds of soldiers on board, and with the help of the Lord and a pair of lucky red undergarments tucked in his pants pocket, he was the ship's new Chief Radio Officer.

# MERCHANT MARINES - 1945

First day out, eager to contribute, Jerry raced to the ship's bow to feel the full force of the wind blowing against his body. The novice marine removed his shirt and tied the sleeves around his neck. With eyes fluttering, hands' palms down, and memories of his childhood, he dreamed again of flying.

By the second day, Jerry remained aft in his narrow bunk bed overcoming onset pneumonia. The weather was of no medicinal help. Masses of clouds and storms caused the carrier to swoop up and down in staggering motion as he crossed the Atlantic. Thirty days were spent along the ocean's highest waves adding daily to the number of sick sailors before finally arriving in England.

But ports of call were a cure-all. Le Havre, Naples, Oran, Malta, Casablanca and Liverpool opened up new worlds to the Chief Radio Officer. Jerry even received a letter from his healthy father, proud that his son was earning $365 per month toiling in German sub-infested waters; and sending ninety percent of the money home to his mother.

Wolman's time in the Merchant Marines was terrifying on occasion. After being re-assigned to a larger troop and munitions carrier, "The Caleb Strong," radio assignments became more chilling at night in the middle of the Atlantic. On one memorable encounter en route to Naples, a German submarine was spotted in the dead center of the convoy. An order of radio silence and "all lights out" immediately went into effect. Despite having left arduous and lengthy duty hours before, as per protocol, Chief Radio Officer Wolman sped in his shorts to the radio room without making a sound.

English cruiser corvettes provided protection surrounding the perimeter of the American troop convoy, and they pursued the unwelcome underwater intruder. The shirtless teenager knelt alone, shuddering in the dark as the sound of dynamite-loaded Ashcan explosives thunderously thumped one after the other. Wolman held tight to steady silence. Not a whimper was emitted from anyone on board during the close and ear-clogging booms. Jerry's thoughts were intense; not about death per se, but focused on the possibility of never seeing his mother and family again. Otherwise his mind during the barrage went blank at each blast.

After what seemed like an elongated out-of-body experience, a message came across the Commodore's ship that the German submarine had been sunk. The transmitted news instantly brought anxiety-releasing cheers, rendered short by the continued duties at hand.

Thankfully, in May 1945, President Roosevelt announced that Germany had surrendered. At that time, Wolman and "The Caleb Strong" crew were headed for Casablanca, a few days to its port. From the radio room, Jerry was able to discover and locate the ship on which his Army brother Bernie was sailing. His vessel was scheduled to leave Casablanca during the same time frame.

Through a minor miracle, the two brothers, each the other's favorite sibling, were able to cross sea-paths, point and wave tearfully to each other and bathe their shouting smiles in Morocco's reddish sunlight. The news of the memorable atypical encounter made front page news in Shenandoah, where both were soon to return.

The Japanese surrendered on the U.S.S. Missouri in September that year. The United States' forces' celebrations at sea were as tumultuous as the oceans in which they were heaving and bobbing. It was not long thereafter that Jerry retired from the Merchant Marines and returned coal-bound to his home town ready to begin the next chapter of his life.

# BERNIE TO ANNE

After the war, Wolman spent an uneventful first year in 1946 on the road. Partnering with a cousin to purchase an International Truck, he began hauling produce from Philadelphia to Shenandoah and its surroundings. The monotony was challenging. Trucking and happiness had become personally incompatible, and eventually came to a final unyielding stop sign.

After being confined to tight ship quarters for so many months, Jerry needed a release and he reunited with his brother Bernie to sow his wild oats. Bernie convinced Jerry to join him in the purchase of a gal-getting, two-door, limo-black Studebaker Land Cruiser with enough chrome to mesmerize any available young woman. The top-of-the-line vehicle cost the then enormous sum of $1100, and the two scratched together every spare and available nickel and dime.

Jerry adored Bernie, his older brother by two years. It was Bernie who had rescued Jerry from the thirteen-year-old's Bar Mitzvah reception. Their father had invited the entire membership of the synagogue to celebrate after Jerry's recitation of his Torah portion. A miserly and meager display of two plain sponge cakes accompanied by a bottle of Old Overholt was for everyone to share. Somehow, Bernie was able to sneak a few small glasses of whiskey to soak the thinly cut cake slices with Jerry. Encouraged by the mixture, the two sped off on a whim, and escaped to New York just hours after the ceremony. Jerry spent his Bar Mitzvah money on his initiation to Broadway, watching "Sons of Fun" starring the famously hilarious duo, Olson and Yolson. Bernie, Jerry and the audience's eyes grew wide in the midst of the on-stage bedlam. The two brothers were inseparable thereafter.

Returning home from war, Bernie had become enveloped in Shenandoah's underlying culture. His taste for whiskey and his propensity to bet on any odds were an ongoing persistent inevitable predicament. Shenandoah's landscape was now dotted with barrooms at every corner and with too many in between. Pool halls abounded with sounds of heavy clicks and illegal gambling parlors were filled with sweating bettors. A dozen patrons in any of the bars bought shots and beers "for the house" as if there were no sobering tomorrow. Jerry stayed by Bernie's side, often helpless to intercede, dabbling with a pool stick, shooting craps and occasionally finding himself caught up in the heavy betting.

One early evening, Jerry and Bernie planned to take the Studebaker to Wilkes-Barre in a shallow, but useful attempt to impress and meet girls. However, along the way, just miles into their trip, the two brothers stopped off at "Henny Kibuilis'," a notorious place of gambling. After an hour of throwing ill-fated dice, with both Bernie and Jerry in the cast, the young men had to make good for some hefty, significant losses. With not nearly enough cash in their pockets, and more than enough unsavory men surrounding them, there was no time for any fancy financing footwork. Having no alternative, Jerry and Bernie forked over their beloved Studebaker to stay alive, and began their journey towards Wilkes-Barre that night by foot.

Of course, no bad luck could stop either brother from searching for dates. After hitching a ride, they scoured for dances and social events in the area. The intrepid pair learned of a wedding party at the Wilkes-Barre Jewish Community Center. They invited themselves and decided to crash. Jerry, who dated frequently but never had the right feeling about any of the girls involved, was always willing to take a risk in the name of romance. Bernie was the first to head for the punch bowl in the hopes it was spiked. He then consumed enough until he had the courage to ask a lady to dance.

Jerry's glance around the Center's reception hall was abbreviated when he saw a young woman who caught his eye. He stared at her for almost a minute. Standing in a mahogany-colored dress cut just below her knees, her beauty instantly reminded him of Gene Tierney, a gifted 1940's movie actress with legs of equally matched talent. As he gazed at her high cheek-bones, Jerry realized that she had an indescribable quality that drew him nearer. She had the sweetest and most caring look about her; more so than anyone he'd ever seen. Jerry ran to grab Bernie, and pointed out the luminous woman across the slick dance floor. "Bernie, I'm going to marry her."

Bernie's guffaw sounded mostly like a liquor-laugh, but he could see Jerry's shoulders backing up, his chest breathing hard and his smile emerging into playfulness. Jerry crossed over to her knowing he would impress.

He asked her name and requested a dance. She replied, "Anne." And while Jerry introduced himself and allowed his teeth to sparkle, they danced until the end of the song. When he immediately asked her for a date, Anne demurely declined. She was, however, willing to let him call her if he wished, and Anne handed over her telephone number without commitment. He was enamored of her sweet and caring tone and even the kindly smell of her perfume. Jerry could also tell that his ball-of-fire approach had met with some soaking.

Anne was on his mind all the way home. He called her a number of times during the week, and finally, she reluctantly agreed to a date. Jerry, then nineteen, and Anne, just seventeen years of age, went to a restaurant called "Knotty Pines" and sat for hours listening to each other. Following his heart's initial sense of love-at-first-sight, Wolman was now with his head in heaven. The two youngsters grew closer and closer after each time together. Jerry was fascinated with her warmth and sensibility. The words and phrases Anne spoke were heartfelt, reliable and spirited.

Over the next months, they talked and laughed as if no other people existed. Soon Anne wanted to be with him always, and even accompanied Jerry on long nighttime driving trips to Philadelphia he had resumed to earn money. She calmed him, caressed him and steadied his very character with her touch. Jerry was exalted, knowing he had met the love of his life. They married on Valentine's Day, February 14th, 1948.

# The Hitch-hiker

The marriage ceremony was held at Anne's father Abe's house in Wilkes-Barre, Pennsylvania, where the penniless couple planned to live temporarily. Abe, following his wife's tragic early death, had become an imperious old coot and was always on the cheap. He wouldn't share a cent for the wedding and bought nothing but day-old bread for the bride, his daughter. Jerry had already opened a fruit and produce stand in Roth's Kosher Meat Market and was making a bare-bones living.

The groom had purchased a wedding ring on credit for $200, a small fortune for the frantic fruit-monger. Anne tearfully called it the most beautiful ring in history. Jerry also purchased a chocolate brown suit for his beautiful bride with a ten dollar deposit on a pay-as-you-go plan so that Anne could be suitably dressed when tying the knot. In the end, Anne and Jerry's glorious living room wedding seemed to them as if they were standing high atop an iced decorated cake.

Unfortunately, within months after the marriage, Jerry's fruit and produce stand began to stagnate. Dejected and broke, he returned to Abe's house after work. Upon opening the door, Jerry found Anne's father screaming viciously at Anne for throwing out some old food. Abe raised his cane in anger over his head as if to strike her. Darting across the room, Jerry jumped to grab the cane from Abe's hand, and broke the hard wooden shaft over his knee. "If you ever touch my wife, I'll beat you to a pulp," Jerry seethed loudly and truthfully. He knew that moment they had to leave. Anne read his mind and affirmed his thoughts.

While packing, the decision on where to go made them uneasy. Jerry presented three choices: Return to Shenandoah, move to Philadelphia or try New York City. Anne didn't want Jerry back driving trucks in Shendo and was hesitant about the bustle and costliness of big cities. After all, they had next to nothing. Jerry listened, and then proposed the craziest gamble of his life. "Let's pick up the first hitch-hiker we see, and wherever he's going, that's where we'll end up." Anne smiled, looked deeply into Jerry's eyes and ventured a glance at his steady grand grin. She believed in him and couldn't resist.

The pair packed their 1938 Chevy with all of the possessions they owned, thereby leaving abundant space for the divining rod hitch-hiker. They drove out of Wilkes-Barre into an area called Mountain Top, and beheld a thumb-out just ahead. The Chevy pulled over to the gravel embankment to possibly allow the stranger in. From the car's window, Jerry asked the unknowing fellow where he was going. "Washington, D.C.," he said. "I'm a student at George Washington University Law School." Jerry and Anne touched hands in the front seat and exhaled with a sigh. "Hop in," they said in unison, "you have a ride."

# Colonial Paint

Six hours later at George Washington University, the Wolmans dropped off their passenger along with their recent past. Famished and aching, they quickly stopped at a Hot Shoppe and shared a syrupy hot fudge sundae for energy. Jerry used his last bit of change to buy a newspaper to peruse the classifieds for available rooms and job listings. They circled a room for rent at 5th and Sheppard Street in Northwest Washington within easy reach and drove with an almost empty tank to meet the owner. Upon arrival, Mrs. O'Hara was waiting at the front door. She seemed as sweet as their last taste of melted ice cream.

Mrs. O'Hara showed the couple a neatly furnished upstairs room and told them the $10 per week rental included kitchen and bathroom privileges. Jerry and Anne admired the graciousness of Mrs. O'Hara and were in desperate need of the room. Uncomfortably, Jerry advised the smiling landlady that there was one minor problem, "We have no money," and looked for her change of expression. But there was none. He continued his hurried off-the-cuff speech into the same smile, "But we've just arrived in town and we'll be able to get jobs tomorrow, to pay you from our first week's paycheck." Mrs. O'Hara replied with more congeniality, "That is a slight problem, not having money, I mean, but I'll certainly trust you for the rent." Using the telephone as if it were a magic wand, she called to the DGS Grocery Store across the street and solemnly declared into the phone's mouthpiece, "Izzy, I've taken on new renters; they're two babes in the woods. Please give them $30 credit for anything they need. I'll guaranty it." She nodded to Jerry and Anne as Izzy complied. "Godsend" was too subtle a word to describe their bold benefactress. And it was no surprise to discover later that Izzy's last name was "Love." That night, the Wolmans slept embracing not only each other, but a future wide open with possibility.

The next morning brought bright sunny prospects. Anne was hired by Prudential Life Insurance Company at her first interview downtown, and started the following Monday in the bookkeeping department. Jerry was hired later in the day by Henry Rubin, the manager of Colonial Wallpaper and Paint Company, at $85 dollars weekly. Wallpaper-trimmer, paint-mixer and counter-man were his titles. Jerry had about as much experience with painting as Tom Sawyer, but feigned knowledge and learned on the job. He spent hours on end absorbing everything there was to know about the inner workings and precision handiwork of the trade. Soon he began honing his salesman skills in earnest.

Jerry let no working moment pass without using his photographic mind. He was the only employee who could ever learn by heart the names of the 1,322 different "Beauty-by-the-Brush" colors, and recognize each as if it were a best friend. In reward, a small raise was given by the store's owners, Phil and Sadie Ackerholt.

Over time, Jerry was made manager and his salary doubled. Shortly thereafter, Anne became pregnant but her carrying was difficult. Jerry insisted she quit her job immediately. Four months later, Anne miscarried to their heartbreak and chagrin. But Jerry's work and drive continued. He took complete control of entirely reorganizing operations. The store's profits quadrupled over the next eighteen months as the enterprise was altered to mirror Jerry's sense of "business not as usual." The young enthusiast was toiling sixteen hours daily, often six days a week.

One memorable night off from work, Jerry took Anne to a baseball game at Griffith Stadium. She was now in a new pregnancy's ninth inning. The World Series Champion Yankees were in Washington to play the Senators, so Jerry and Anne weathered the night's rain to admire the play of Phil Rizzuto, Yogi Berra and the celebrated Yankee Clipper, Joe DiMaggio. As if lightning had been struck, the crowd marveled in awe at DiMaggio's powerfully glorious barrage, smashing three towering home runs over the ballpark's fence; the most ever by any player at Griffith Stadium. And on the very next day, Rosh Hashana, lightning struck again. Helene Marsha Wolman was born on September 12th, 1950 at 4:00 a.m. On the Jewish holiday that symbolizes the New Year and hope for good things in the year ahead, Jerry could not have felt more blessed. His wife and daughter doing well, Jerry considered himself lucky to have become a father and decent provider with a career in place for opportunity to grow. He adored Anne with incalculable emotion, and the baby with a new feeling of paternal ferocity. His swagger around Helene's crib was pronounced by his doting love, pride and sense of privilege.

The proud mother was equally overjoyed. In a letter to her beautiful newborn daughter, Anne wrote these words:

*"To my little Helene,*

*You have brought your Daddy and me the greatest joy that two people could ever hope for. My wish for you is that you grow up to be a good girl, in good health, and that you're a well-liked, happy girl. You're named after two very wonderful people and if you follow in their footsteps, you'll be alright. May God grant you everything that your heart desires, but Helene, don't be selfish, think of others, and try to bring happiness into the lives of other people.*

*I love you dearly,*

*Your Mother"*

\*\*\*\*\*

Early on at Colonial, Wolman had been promised that a bonus was coming to him near the end of his first year as manager. It didn't arrive. He was then told by Mr. Ackerholt that "he was family" and would be given stock in the company so that he could more equitably share in the profits he'd catapulted. A mere bonus was inadequate according to Phil. The elderly Ackerholts had no children, and implied that Jerry would eventually buy out the remaining stock from them and one day own the corporation. The stock transfer, however, seemed always around the proverbial corner.

Anne and Jerry had already moved to an efficiency apartment at $60 per month after their long-ago initial raises; but with business beginning to bulge and promises of ownership in hand, and with Helene gurgling gleefully, the new parents had the highest hopes of proprietary rights for their own family. Only the Ackerholts' unkept promises were acting as roadblocks. Profits continued to zoom as Jerry was enticed and inspired to work harder than ever.

One afternoon, an unannounced pain closing in on his chest, followed by numbness up and down his arm, brought Jerry to Dr. Paul A. Lichtman. Only the wisest of physicians would have known to complement a thorough medical exam with a candid conversation of Jerry's lifestyle and aspirations. Good Dr. Lichtman assured Jerry that his heart was medically fine, but could only mend if he received in life that to which he was entitled. His fatherly physician's advice was to move far away from anyone whose promises were not scrupulously kept. "Never trust someone whose word is empty," prescribed the doctor.

Wolman emerged from Dr. Lichtman's office feeling pain-free and unusually strong. He called Phil Ackherholt from a payphone and asked for a meeting. They met at the store where Jerry explained he was leaving, and would stay only until his replacement arrived. Phil's forehead moistened and his lips quivered. He offered an immediate bonus and prompt calls to attorneys to finalize the stock transaction "right after the tax season." Dr. Lichtman's words rang true in Jerry's ears. The trust for Ackerholt was forever gone and Jerry no longer had patience for delays fueled by lies. An emboldened Jerry felt powerful in declining.

At age twenty-three, the young father and budding entrepreneur started his own painting company, promising himself never to treat others as he had been treated. There and then he vowed to make certain he'd always do the opposite, forever acknowledging his wife's powerful words passed on and embedded in the gentle letter to his newborn daughter.

# Painting To Building - 1951

Painting a three-story apartment building's three hundred windows was excruciating work for a sole practitioner with little more than hand-brushes. Starting his first job, Wolman had no money to purchase scaffolding, sturdy ladders or help. But a nice widow who owned a series of apartments was willing to compensate Jerry for doing so at his asking price of $2,500. His broad shoulders to a swinging grindstone, Jerry hung perilously from an old rickety extension ladder. Balancing to accomplish the detailed work on the second and third floor casings, he was not without his memory of childhood flight. The satisfied widow paid him the full sum due as soon as the paint had dried. The lone, lanky craftsman believed he had scraped, primed, brushed and painted his way to the pot of gold at the end of a personal rainbow. It was the largest payday he'd ever known.

Business began bustling as home builders heard of his dependable, quality workmanship. Word-of-mouth spread his reputation quickly and soon he was able to hire a half-dozen helpers whom he prodded jovially toward perfection. The workmanship was first-rate, and builders' payments were dependable. Yet something inside Jerry was missing.

Watching the building process fascinated Jerry all the way back from the time he began as a manager at Colonial. While struggling to cut wall-paper to size one afternoon, out of the corner of his eye, he noticed a construction site across the street from the store. Jerry couldn't help but get distracted as a structure grew fitfully out of the ground. From what had recently been an empty lot, a building's shape emerged in outline form with underground ditches and poured concrete. Weeks later, he watched the pipes and frames appear as the building's character grew upward and gained width. He soon found himself face against the store's window utterly fixated when all was positioned to measure the weight of bricks and mortar and siding. Finally the roof was in place, and to Jerry's astonishment and elation while working late into the night, the building's interior lights went on all at once. The next day, he wandered across the street for a closer look, and spied as he conversed with workers about his Colonial's paint products and wallpaper.

Now out painting newly-constructed homes on his own, Jerry's curiosity once again began to pique. Captivated, he perceived that the construction of a home entailed a series of interlocking puzzle pieces which required the co-ordination of men, time and space. As Jerry painted in areas of new development with houses being built around him, he paid strict attention. On Sundays, Jerry and Anne, with extra cotton diapers for Helene, began driving back to the site to view the development's progression. Off hours, he continued his weekend visitations to a number of home-building sites, sometimes alone in feverish contemplation. He began to memorize and analyze each project's beginnings, middles and ends. Jerry never hesitated, as always, to offer his services as a most adept painter whenever he could, but his demeanor was now consumed with almost religious observance of a home's constructive birth.

Jerry's mind was as set as a block of hardened smooth cement. His painting days, he realized, were coming close to an end. He wanted to become a builder. With little money, no education or experience, determination was his best asset. He recalled that such a trait had never failed him in the past.

As if on cue, Mort "Ugly" Lippman, a close-by competitor of Colonial's paint business, told Jerry that he had a piece of ground for sale at 53rd and B Street in Southeast Washington. He wanted $5,000 for it, and added that it was zoned for 16 apartments. Jerry yearned to make the deal and asked for a few days to raise the money. From where, Jerry did not know. Suddenly he recalled Garrett Pendleton, a frequent customer at Colonial with whom he'd become friendly when he was employed there. Mr. Pendleton also happened to be a commercial loan officer at nearby McLachen Bank.

Jerry went to Mr. Pendleton at McLachen's offices, brought the banker up to date and explained what he was trying to do. Pendleton listened with interest. He always liked Jerry's amicable nature and held respect for the young man's tireless work ethic. He had observed with his own bank-view how Jerry had run the Colonial company business single-handedly and handily with utter honesty and much success. Poker-faced, Jerry asked for and explained why he needed a $5,000 loan.

Mr. Pendleton asked that Jerry provide him with a financial statement so that the loan officer could take it to the board. Jerry knew less about financial statements than he had initially about slicing wallpaper to size. He could only figure it out by trial and error, until perfect. Without an ounce of trepidation, Jerry prepared the most detailed statement of his finances for the board's review. He returned to Mr. Pendleton the next morning. The banker chuckled at the listings. Jerry had included his clothing, the tie-clip he was wearing, his household utensils and even the wedding band on his ring-finger that tapped along the edge of Pendleton's desk.

While pointing out one of the statement's finer financial points, Jerry's other hand brushed a penny that had been scattered among some change on the desk. Without hesitation, Jerry bent down and crawled deeply underneath the furniture to retrieve the shiny coin. He placed the penny back on the desk while the color and composure returned to his face. Mr. Pendleton succinctly uttered, "You have the loan. Any man who would worry as much about one tiny penny of mine is also going to worry about repaying my loan."

"There's one condition," he added, as Jerry's rakish smile froze. "If you're ever going to make a late payment, let me know beforehand, so that I can make it for you. I'm sticking my neck out that far." Jerry again jumped out of his chair, but this time only to shake hands with the loan officer. And with one precious penny, Jerry Wolman's building career began.

# LOANS

"**D**on't do it," insisted his closest friends. "Impossible," was their advice. Constructing a four-building apartment complex with four family flats each was unimaginable to any of them. Jerry admitted their point, but was driven by his dream. So he bought the empty land, but before he could build, first he needed to secure additional financing. To his surprise, the near impossible task involved securing two types: a permanent and a construction loan.

Jerry made continuous applications for a loan to build his project. The first twenty-five rejections came almost daily. Then it got harder. Months and months passed, with turn-down upon unrequited turn-down. After meeting with every lender in the nation's capital he went to New York, only to meet with similar reviews. With no knowledge of building and an empty resume, he exited each appointment in disappointment. But he was never deterred. Forced to maintain his painting business to pay the Pendleton loan without fail, he could barely make ends meet. As that year of rejections went by, his shirt collar felt as if it were contracting with each passing month.

The heat in the pressure cooker Jerry found himself left the scales of Fahrenheit when his son Alan was born on a boiling August 13th, 1952. Jerry always wanted a son; one that looked just like him. Upon Alan's birth, Anne quickly handed the newborn infant to her husband and said, "Well, you've got your boy." Overjoyed at the birth of a son yet overwrought by the endless slamming of his financial plans, Jerry was deliriously happy and just as deliriously desperate for money. He soon realized first, that his son was the spitting image of Anne, and that second, more than ever, he needed a larger place for his family to live.

Jerry was able to finagle-swap the purchase of a new house from a builder whose liquidity was being drained by the omnipresent recession. Max Miller owed Jerry the last payment on a painting job that Jerry had completed weeks before. "Just pay me when you can," forgave Jerry despite his own hard times. Jerry then figured a possible trade. He suggested to Max that he would call the amount owed "even" if Jerry could take over the payments on the house that Max had just built at 334 Oglethorpe Street in Northeast Washington. Max thought the transaction to be a benefit to both men and agreed.

Anne was filled with joy owning her own home, with space for the children to run around at will. She hugged her husband for days on end. But even those embraces were insufficient to alleviate the fear of failing his growing obligations including mortgage payments, utilities and tax bills. Nonetheless, Jerry was unfailing in his perseverance, growing more convinced he'd get the loan he needed despite the dry economic atmosphere.

In the early 1950's the economy had been lulled to sleep by an inattentive Truman administration more worried about Communism in general and specifically with insurgent North Koreans threatening civil war. The joke was, in bars back in hard-pressed Shenandoah, a beer without a head was now called "a Truman." Jerry saw interest rates for building loans in Washington reach an apex, close to 20 percent. Scattered vacant lots opened up all around. Wolman's relatives saw the bountiless builder dragging and bereft, with no results for his nearly two years of persistence. They begged him to stay away from building anything, let alone an apartment complex as his lot in life.

*****

Elizabeth II had her coronation as Queen of England in 1952 and Dwight D. Eisenhower had his inauguration as President of the United States in 1953 before Jerry Wolman had his first permanent construction loan. His final luck was primed by his disciplined preparation. While hammering the streets for a year and a half, Jerry pieced together his construction team. He knew he didn't know, and was smart enough to ask around for the right people to guide him. In that fashion, he discovered the best architect to handle the type of housing he had in mind. He learned from others that a successful developer must hire the services of the finest bricklayers, the best plumbers and the most competent electricians. Jerry prepared to do so. He also was able to get a promise from a construction maven and skilled bricklayer, Nick Romano, on a handshake, to start work for Jerry as soon as the loan was apprehended. Likewise with another handshake, Jerry was able to entice Benjamin Krick, an outstanding contractor, to handle all the plumbing. Sub-contractors lined up when they learned of Jerry's selections.

The hunt for the permanent loan ended in Canada where lending for huge loans was far looser. A Washington D.C. broker who was the correspondent for Sun Life of Canada reviewed Jerry's loan package with him. It included the names of the experienced craftsman he had lined up, the expenses for each, and the prospective rental income of the apartments, unit by unit. The correspondent was impressed and round-tripped to and from the northern country, returning with a Canadian goose that had just laid a golden egg: $90,000 for Jerry's permanent loan. Exultant, but with one more hurdle to jump: the construction loan, Jerry returned to Mr. Pendleton for renewed advice. Wolman had spent another five months attempting to nail down the elusive starter loan when Pendleton sent him to an acquaintance of his, Johnny Beale at Security Bank.

Beale had the personality of a worm in a rotten apple, wriggling with inquiries of Jerry's lack of qualifications. All his questions were answered honestly and quickly. However, Security's sentinel was pessimistic the bank would make the money available to him.

"But leave your stuff here; I'll get back to you in a week."

Wolman believed that Mr. Pendleton intervened on his behalf, for when a week concluded, Beale called him at home, "Wolman, come down here." The would-be builder raced.

Jerry sat motionless with knuckles ivory-tusk-white across from Mr. Beale. "I got your loan for you," he grunted. Jerry leapt uncontrollably and kissed him full on the lips. The starchy startled banker blinked but never smiled, and remained otherwise motionless.

"Let's get this closed," he stammered. For Jerry Wolman, it was finally time to build.

Settlement occurred as Wolman signed all documents without reading a word. Construction began with the digging of dirt for pouring the foundation. The cement truck could have been pouring euphoria instead of concrete. With bull-dozers scraping and unloading the earth, the new builder threw a silver dollar for burial into the first ditch being covered with cool gray lava. Jewish tradition maintains that by planting the silver seed, the foundation would sprout not only an edifice, but fortune as well.

Nick Romano was a hard-nosed foreman who met Jerry every morning between 5:00 and 6:00 a.m. to discuss the ongoing progress. Jerry pushed Nick, and Nick pushed all contractors in concert.

Every contractor was offered a bonus to complete work at the speed of light. Providing goals for the workers to make money saved Jerry much more on balance. Paying interest on a lagging job was a wasted dollar. And needless to say, no rental checks would be forthcoming from tenants until occupancy. So Jerry pushed forward until a startling dilemma arose.

Romano failed to appear. Jerry called his home, but his wife did not know his whereabouts. As other subs on the job arrived hours later, they advised Jerry that Nick was not unknown to disappear three or four times a year "on a toot." But perhaps the vanishing act by his crew chief was a blessing. Faced with no alternative, Jerry became his own foreman, running Nick's bricklayers, commandeering the plumbers and exhorting the electricians. He asked questions as often as necessary, but listened intensely when those with more knowledge than he spoke. In the beginning of his adventure at complete control, he never asked a question for which he knew the answer. As his knowledge grew, he began to ask only those questions that could improve work function. He noticed that bricklayers would lose almost two hours each day waiting until laborers stocked up the decks with brick, block and mixing mortar.

Jerry took matters in his own calloused hands. He remained on site an extra four or five hours at the end of each work day stocking up the decks himself with brick and block. It was back-breaking loneliness, but no more so than loading ten tons of produce onto a truck. At back-breaking brawn, Jerry was the expert. Discounting more time, he also arrived two hours before anyone each morning to mix the mortar himself. He carried it alone in a heavy hod up onto decks into mortar pans. Jerry supplied it all with his massive effort below a sunset or sunrise.

Nick Romano returned after a month, and neither Jerry nor he said a word to each other about his absence. They just kept on working as if nothing had happened.

Bricklayers beamed as their work product tripled. They bore down even harder in anticipation of their bonuses and in utter admiration for the stamina and skill of the kid from Shenandoah. No one believed it could be accomplished when tenants started moving in within three months of the day the silver dollar was deposited. Wolman had so much pride that he considered keeping the property. However, needing the money for his next project, he had no choice but to sell it.

He placed an ad in the newspaper with a picture of the buildings taken in the rain. For reasons incomprehensible to all but developers, buildings always looked better as pictured in rain.

The first call was from a Chinese restaurateur who owned an eatery called SIWO on Kennedy Street in Washington. He was no easy pickings. The Chinese gentleman hemmed and hawed proclaiming that he wasn't sure the buildings were to his liking. Jerry became determined to take the slow boat to Chinatown. He ate Chinese food at SIWO for weeks gaining a relationship with its owner. Jerry ate every item from every column on the menu. He returned day after day until his fortune cookies finally foretold a sale.

The Chinaman purchased two buildings for $36,000 each and came to closing with bags of cash. Shortly thereafter, Jerry sold the other two buildings for similar amounts, netting $40,000 from the project. Wolman realized that his three months' work had returned more profit than he'd ever seen. A young rascal from the coal region of Pennsylvania with less than a high school education had managed to earn what seemed a monster sum of money.

Tasting success, Wolman immediately moved his mother and father to a home he purchased for them in Washington, just a few blocks away from a shul. His mother never had anything which meant so much to her. Her glow of happiness was precious to Jerry. And his fabulous smile in return was her greatest joy.

# A Promise Kept

No hiatus could be short enough for Wolman to purchase another lot, this time in nearby bordering Virginia. Figuring his recent success would alleviate any difficulty in future financing, he purchased a property upon sight without contingencies. But those elusive loans proved just as difficult to gain. When the note on the realty quickly came due, he sweated bullets contemplating default. Non-payment would have curtailed his building efforts out of existence.

While pondering the problem, he drove by a new development under construction which caught his eye. He stopped and stepped inside. Jerry was enthralled by each apartment's modern layout which included abundantly large closets and windows in both the kitchen and bathrooms. After reading the architect's name and address from the outdoor construction sign, Jerry swiftly appeared at his office. Short, but sizably confident, Edmund W. Dreyfuss was a remarkable architect who accepted the challenge of structuring a loan transaction with his seasoned sources. As the two initially shook hands, a lasting bond had formed. Dreyfuss continued to design almost all of Wolman's future buildings, becoming not only a key business partner, but a dear lifelong friend.

Having learned a bit from his first profit-maker, Jerry employed as many of the same contractors as were available, using his "bonus" and "early morning/late evening preparation" systems to coordinate the readiness of his construction. He also hired his first engineer and land surveyor, Calvin B. Burns, whose expertise solved every state and county permit problem. Interestingly, while at work on the site, Burns discovered a peculiar marker in the ground. After some "digging," it was determined the marker had been originally placed by surveyor George Washington as the outer boundary of Washington, D.C. The Daughters of the American Revolution applauded the find, verified it, and put a spritely open fence around the marker where it remains to this day. The value of the lot was enhanced, and the discovery gave rental agents a story to tell for quicker leasing. Completing in record time, the sale of the Patrick Henry Heights project in Seven Corners, Virginia netted the wowed Wolman $150,000 in profits in 1954.

*****

Alexandria, Virginia was a fancier location for Jerry's next lesson-filled venture. The zoning permitted four three-story buildings totaling sixty units, but common sense told Jerry to erect only three buildings and save the corner. He surmised that after the three were up, the alluring extra land would be worth more than he was about to pay for the entire property, $72,000 in cash. In order to purchase, he required a partner with a mountain of a financial statement. Jack Slan, a retired wealthy former grocer filled the need. Jack was good with numbers, and after seeing the fiscal beauty of the deal, he was willing to be a fairly silent partner. Financing the permanent and construction loans was still drudgery, but Slan's million dollar financial statement melted the heart of Frank Hight, a member of the firm of Bogley, Harting and Hight. The firm provided the Wolman/Slan partnership a $270,000 commitment from its lending entity.

Jerry already had his plans, permits and subs lined up ready to roll, but Frank Hight's primary concern was the un-built corner lot. At closing, Jerry told him they were reserving it, hopeful that after the three apartment buildings were complete, it could be sold off as a gas station, a perfect fit.

Hight grimaced and gritted his teeth, "I could not have my lenders make this loan if they knew that a gas station would front the apartment complex they were financing. The offer will be withdrawn unless I have your word that no gas station will go there."

Jack and Jerry discussed the dilemma and hastily gave Frank Hight their word that they would build only what had been pre-approved by Hight on the corner piece. Frank said, "Fine, as long as I have your word, I'll wrap up the loans."

Construction began as Slan went on a month-long vacation. Speed and efficiency moved matters along as if the site were an automobile production line. Then Slan returned from his respite in Florida and wanted to meet Wolman. Slan had a contract in hand that he'd negotiated at poolside purporting to sell the corner lot for $72,000. Just as Jerry was about to sign on the dotted line, he asked a wildly excited Slan to whom he'd sold the land. "To Shell, the gas station company," Slan gloated.

"Did you clear it with Frank Hight?" Jerry inquired less heartily.

"No." replied Slan loudly, and then with greater amplification, "We don't need his approval; he has nothing in writing from us!"

"Jack, we can't do that," Jerry swallowed. "We gave Frank our word."

"You can take your word and ten cents and go buy a cup of coffee!" hollered his irate partner.

The ensuing argument seemed endless until Jerry demanded that they at least call Hight and plead their case. After all, Jerry needed the money more than Jack. Perhaps Hight would relent because half the properties were leased without a hitch in the developer's performance. They called, and in a short and stern conversation, Hight reminded the pair of the oral promise he expected to be kept. Nodding his head, Jerry reiterated the promise and hung up the phone.

Jack Slan became ballistic at the click of the receiver. He accused his younger partner of idiocy and having no comprehension as to how business is done. He threatened Jerry viciously that if his signature was not forthcoming on the contract, they were finished. But it was too late. Jerry had already agreed they were finished and Jack Slan stormed out.

A separation seemed more than appropriate, so Jerry suggested a silent auction buy-out on the fourth lot. Jack cautioned Jerry and offered to personally guarantee financing for the next Wolman project if Jerry would simply allow the gas station sale.

In the end, Jack bought Jerry out on the corner lot, but only after Wolman legally restricted his former partner in writing: nothing but an apartment building could ever be built or sold on that land.

The three primary buildings of The Hume Springs were completed in the meantime, with exquisite profits after they were leased and sold. Nevertheless, Slan remained furious at his former partner's good deed, and decided to show him up by building an apartment complex himself on the corner as his own general contractor. Within days of digging the foundation, Slan hit the very springs of Hume Springs. Jerry had been lucky enough to miss any underground water for the first three buildings, but Slan's misfortune required swimming lessons. He called Wolman and begged him to bail him out. Reluctantly, Jerry accepted finishing the project, and when it was done, the two men never spoke again. Out of Frank Hight's office, word spread all over town of Wolman's impeccable integrity, which in turn benefited his continued ascent in the real estate business world. After Hume Springs, Jack Slan never made another deal.

With Hume Springs finalized in all respects by late 1955, now splashing in money, Jerry was more ambitious than ever. Parlaying land owned by a neighbor, Izzy Hoffberg, and Judge Nathaniel Ely, Jerry was easily able to finance The Glenn Ross Apartments in Silver Springs, Maryland. He labored on as his partners watched the construction of 166 garden apartment units rise with lightning alacrity and peerless workmanship. The partnership profited over $350,000 of which Wolman retained an agreed staggering $150,000 sum.

Jerry was now so well self-educated in the planning, financing and development of garden apartment complexes that he could list in his mind in three dimensions his cost for the land, the bricks and mortar, and the charges for plumbing, carpentry and other major sub-contractors. Simultaneously, his cerebrum created the rental possibilities for each unit and how quickly they would be leased. He calculated in milliseconds his pricing for the eventual sale of the entire complex based upon interest rates at the time of completion. Instantaneously the profit was displayed before his eyes as if he had been able to use a computer. Jerry liked what he saw on his mind's screen and reveled with delight over his creations. It was apparent. Apartment buildings were his forte and niche.

# The Soft-hearted Home-builder

*"If Jerry Wolman was born a girl, he'd have been pregnant all the time."*

-Joe King, former Business Manager for the Philadelphia Eagles

*****

Jerry Wolman learned that a soft heart and success can easily coexist, but may not always coexist with ease. One way or another, he found extreme difficulty saying "no."

One dream he'd not yet conquered was a home-building project. The construction of homes after all is what had fascinated him as a painter. Within months, the opportunity arose to create 138 single-family homes, a massive undertaking in Fairfax, Virginia. Confident now after having chomped off and thoroughly chewed reliably profitable apartment developments, he viewed the upcoming homes as challenging, but certainly well within his expertise.

When building apartments, prospective tenants were rarely at or involved in his previous sites, and Jerry had complete control, being beholden to no one. However, Wolman soon discovered that constructing single-family homes was altogether a much different endeavor. To-be-homeowners proved to-be-meddlesome. Jerry's jobs had previously been met with machine-like co-ordination. Now they were being met with the picky personal preferences and problems of 138 different families.

After a few of the houses were up and soon to be ready, Jerry made one costly concession, revealing a sympathetic side to his soul. One woman on a weekend visit to her almost finished home, stood at her front door step crying. While crossing the turf of her lawn, she saw Jerry approaching his office/trailer. He immediately asked why she was tearful. She sobbed, now also slobbering, that she had chosen the wrong door. She didn't like it, and wanted the one with a small paned window with all grained wood, not paint. Jerry checked his paperwork and the door was what had been previously selected. He showed the woman her choice. She screamed, "I can't live with it!" she wept with her hands covering her face.

"Look", said Jerry unable to feel anything but his heart swelling, "I'll do you a favor; I want you to feel better, so do me a favor and please stop crying. At my cost, I'll upgrade your door so that it's exactly what you want."

Jerry felt warm all over when the woman turned her wet frown into a puffy-lipped smile. Jerry's new foreman, Frank Bolek, replaced the door the next day while the woman and her neighbors watched. Later that afternoon, a line of women began to form outside Jerry's mobile office. Bolek didn't know what to do. One complained that the perfectly laid flooring appeared uneven, while another demanded her door swing the other way. More and more ridiculous items were added to the growing punch lists. No matter how large they grew and no matter how ridiculous, Jerry told Frank Bolek to fix all requests without question.

"Don't even argue about it," he ordered.

Wolman unfortunately lost a bundle on his first housing project. Though he owed his workmen a sizeable sum at its finish, he'd been generous with them on their previous jobs. To a man, they empathized with their beleaguered good-hearted employer. Helping him avoid a career catastrophe, Jerry's workers remained loyal and patiently waited for him to pay off all of his bills over time. These subcontractors who risked their necks for the young builder were rewarded exponentially as they embarked with Wolman down a glorious road.

In the final analysis, Jerry managed to lose money on a project for the very first time. But in doing so, he also managed to win the happiness of 138 young, decent, working families. Wolman also learned a valuable lesson about being openhandedly generous with his men, as one never knows when he'll need that same generosity in return.

*****

Years later, Wolman would look back and ironically point out, *"The only time I never lost money building single-family homes was when I built houses for friends at cost!"*

# Building Wealth

In the mid-1950's, Wolman purchased a number of vacant pieces of real estate on which to build apartments and office buildings. Prior to settlement, the land had appreciated so much in value, that he began to sell the naked site to others at a substantial profit before any worker had set foot upon it. This type of winning move in an up real estate market is called a "flip." Soon Jerry was flipping properties as if they were griddled pancakes. Also, Wolman's domain of realized development properties was expanding exponentially. As half the decade ended, Wolman's net worth, professional acumen and good heart were the envious objects of every real estate investor's conversations.

Jerry had to trade in his portable filing system's metal can and cabinet in exchange for his first real office. What had been the basement of Gusti's restaurant on M Street in Northwest Washington was now serving up Jerry's architectural plans, loan applications and blue print specials. As operations grew, Jerry needed help and moved his brother Manny down from Shenandoah into the new digs to manage the burgeoning Jerry Wolman Construction Company.

Wolman always realized the importance of having knowledgeable people around him. From the beginning, he treated those who worked hard for him with a sense of family. Oftentimes blurring the lines between business and family, he routinely opened his heart and home to his workmen on holidays and get-togethers, even delving on occasion closely into their personal lives. As Jerry's success blossomed, he began a most unorthodox habit rarely seen in the business world. He consistently rewarded those underneath him with bonuses, almost always sharing portions of his profits. He knew loyal people were the key to working in sync with his immense drive and need for precision. He simply wanted others to derive joy and prosperity from their success.

During the exasperating homebuilding effort, foreman Nick Romano once again disappeared. Jerry's operation was in temporary disarray. He adjusted promptly to entrust a gritty workman whose durability and know-how had impressed him. Literally pulling Frank Bolek off the bulldozer that day, Jerry made him superintendent over the project. This key promotion proved to help solidify Jerry's tenacious team. But no addition to that team, however, was more significant than Ted Dailey.

In the spring of 1957, with growing confidence, Jerry bought a property near the University of Maryland named Magruder Park. Almost the same day, he was approached by a dentist, Irving Lichtman, the brother of the physician who had advised Jerry to start his own business. The dentist seemed sharp and had fine banking connections, admirable and necessary attributes for a business relationship with Jerry. They began to discuss partnering on the project and shook hands to do so.

When the purchase of Magruder Park found its way into the newspapers, Jerry received a telephone call which would change his business dealings forever. On the other end of the line was Ted Dailey, who had just been hired to head the commercial loan department for The Rouse Company and wanted to meet Wolman at his new office.

There was something about the stocky, five-foot four inch, bushy eye-browed, good Catholic father of twelve that Jerry liked. Dailey badly wanted to broker and obtain the financing on Magruder Park for The Rouse Company, which at the time was interested in moving into the commercial property market. After conferring with Lichtman on all the numbers in Dailey's presence, an application was signed. In less than three days, Dailey was back with a commitment for exactly what was needed, plus some additional favorable terms.

Jerry was about to pay the requested $5,000 fee to Dailey and lock in the rates when his phone rang. Jerry shared his delight at

Ted's fine work, when Lichtman yelled so loudly that Jerry's hand shook from the swirl of the sound vibrating near his ear. "Don't sign anything!" the voice insisted. Lichtman felt sure he could best Dailey's transaction by $10,000. But Jerry remained adamant, explaining that Mr. Dailey, who was seated in front of him, had traveled and worked hard for the past 72 hours, and had met and even exceeded all of their terms.

"We cannot do things like that," he lectured the dentist. The Lichtman-Wolman battle was knockdown drag out. This was the second venture-partner to whom Jerry had to explain what to him was a no-brainer.

"I'm doing the right thing," Jerry commanded to overrule him. But Lichtman would have none of it, and said he'd buy Jerry out. Wolman agreed on the spot, wanting nothing more to do with him. When the cantankerous conversation ended, Jerry hung up the phone, and then wrote a check for $5,000 to the order of Ted Dailey still sitting across from him.

"You've earned it," Wolman smiled in earnest as he pushed the check into Dailey's hands. Ted never forgot that gesture and became Jerry's tireless loan correspondent. During Ted's career representing Jerry Wolman, he placed for him, in one form or another, over $500,000,000 in loans. Dailey's friendship and loyalty were even more valuable. Of course, Jimmy Rouse's commercial loan portfolio didn't do so badly, having struck a veritable vein of gold.

# Friends And Neighbors

Anne stepped out on the porch with her arms folded just above her waist-high apron. She'd started roasting her brisket over onions by mid-afternoon next to a pot of chicken soup simmering with matzo balls on the stove. Anne watched proudly as her friends and family played in the yard. Seven-year old Helene and five year-old Alan were having fun with the neighbor's kids, while Jerry verbally jousted with the youngster's parents.

"Food will be ready in ten," Anne said softly and smiled at Jerry, who took a drag of his cigarette and winked at her.

Simple weekend days like these made Anne Wolman the most happy. Unaffected by her husband's recent success, she took genuine pleasure in people joining her and sharing good fortune. As Anne looked on at her husband's good-humored camaraderie with his next door buddies, and heard the giggles of high-spirited children, she felt blessed to have moved into a home surrounded by the close friendships of such genuine people. It was no coincidence, however, that everyone who lived in their immediate vicinity happened to get along so well. It was all pre-planned in Jerry's friendly neighborhood blue prints.

Wolman had met and become friendly with his neighbors through a game of poker two years earlier. A friend of a friend had asked Jerry to fill an empty seat one evening at Mel Lenkin's card game. As Jerry counted his chips before play, he peeked around the table at his opponents' starched white shirts and uncalloused hands holding finer brands of smokes. Intimidated, the usually boisterous prankster sat in silence surrounded by conversation swirling in directions unfamiliar to him. Shenandoah felt ten thousand miles away. Soon Jerry began to grow more confident with each chip raise. He kept returning each week to the rotating game and in no time became the most vocal at the table. Jerry grew fond of the men who readily accepted him in return and began to feel no differences between them. Each had young children of similar ages, and when the men's wives also got friendly, Wolman investigated the idea of building something he'd never thought of before: his own community of friends.

In the fall of 1956 Jerry purchased plentiful plots of ground in Chevy Chase, Maryland for himself as well as several of his regular card-buddies. Feeling much richer after having sold a particularly successful apartment building, and enjoying his close core of new friends, he decided to construct houses on four of the lots: one for his family, and three more to include the families of Stanley Reines, Jack Geller and Bob Kasnett.

Jerry built and sold the luxurious homes to these dearest friends at his cost, and then arranged to find them mortgages in excess of the purchase price so that all could walk away from closing with a few extra thousands in cash. Over the years the families lived amiably, enjoying each other. They shared countless afternoons eating cold-cut platters and Sloppy Joe's, and playfully engaging in recreation at each other's back yards and front lawns.

Among the men wearing starched white shirts at one of Jerry's card games was a young D.C. lawyer named Earl Foreman. Polished and reserved, Earl impressed Jerry as a smart and decent fellow. The two shared common ground when the topic of sports was raised, and when Wolman heard that Earl was an avid fan, a certain chemistry formed. In between hands dealt, Jerry learned that Earl specialized in the handling of real estate transactions and Wolman retained Foreman to represent him at his next closing. Foreman's fee was in the range of $5,000, but Jerry was so delighted at the speed and proficiency of the real estate settlement that he upped the ante by an additional $2,000.

After one or two more poker games and smooth closings, Earl's extra bonuses grew larger. Foreman knew how to get a deal closed, and the more Jerry paid Earl, the more preference he then gave to Jerry. Soon Jerry Wolman effectively became Earl's sole concentration. With each taste of success, Jerry continued to sweeten Earl's deals by rewarding his side-kick attorney with ownership interests, usually in the 10% range. Such proffered gratuities gave the attorney the opportunity to make substantial sums of money, plus accumulate considerable tax benefits, all to his advantage.

The two men became inseparable, almost like brothers as their symbiotic careers rose congruently together. Jerry's sense of humor and Earl's consistently cordial contacts with other attorneys created fast opportunities for business transactions interlaced with good times. Earl Foreman began to loosen his tightly-knotted necktie because he never really quite knew what to expect from Jerry Wolman. As 1956 came to an enviably prosperous close, Earl found a 1957 Cadillac Chanukah gift in his driveway outside his home. Incredulous at the magnanimous present, Earl sat inside his lavish holiday bonus and steered around the streets of Washington in self-congratulatory style. For years thereafter, Foreman made himself available to Jerry day and night, ready at Wolman's beck and call. And those calls came often as Jerry's career was reaching an apex of one or two solid construction deals per month. Seated upon and fastened into Wolman's success and extraordinary generosity, Earl Foreman was riding high.

# Summit Hill

With Foreman, Dailey, Bolek and Dreyfuss in perpetual racing pace, Wolman was about to build his first high rise apartment building on a hasty, hearty handshake. Through 1959, Jerry had completed hundreds of low rise (three floors or less) garden apartments as if by contractors with heavy mechanized cookie-cutters. Wolman used his mathematically profit-driven eyes to see and take the risks of purchase. Dailey obtained financing and loans at favorable rates. Dreyfuss maintained the design of units with enlarged closets, windows-in-kitchen-and-bath heightened by tall ceilings. Bolek supervised construction with savvy oversight, visiting every project daily and meeting Wolman frequently to co-ordinate the arrivals of supplies and workmen. Foreman then culled together the attorneys and principals for buyers or sellers, lenders and title companies so that settlements for purchases and sales were quick and painless.

Penn Gardens' 1200 units, Pembroke Gardens' 400 units, Starcrest's 516 units, Suncrests' 232 units and literally over dozens more sites were ongoing at the same time over the early heydays. It did not take Jerry long, however, to calculate that *high* rises of nine or more floors could triple or quadruple the number of units on the same plot of ground, given zoning and permit approvals.

Jerry saw a sweet, choice property at the corner of 16th Street and East West Highway called "Snow Tract" advertised for auction. He knew immediately that a high rise here could sustain 1100 residential units, and it was already zoned for 1200, plus a small shopping center and an office building. Use of the land's thirty acres upon which huge trees swayed and riding trails meandered would be first class and super deluxe.

Wolman and an astute young land speculator named Nick Basiliko were the two still bidding as the auctioneer accepted raised-hand bids above half a million dollars. Jerry set his limit at $600,000 and made his last head-nod at that figure. Basiliko topped it with an intimidating $630,000 knock-down-awarding bid.

Disappointed to despair, Jerry was unable to sleep that night as he tossed and turned with the numbers as if counting profiteering sheep. He acknowledged in his dreams that he had lost out on a chance of a lifetime. Upon awakening, he called Basiliko to meet. That afternoon the pair convened at Nick's office where Wolman offered to buy Nick's contract for $100,000 over the auction price. Nick boldly countered with a hefty jump to $350,000 over his day-old bid. Jerry courteously declined, but showed Nick the rental unit financial figures and possibilities if Jerry's team were to build the high rise. Basiliko was fascinated with the math and knew of Jerry's prowess. A 50/50 deal was offered to the speculator so long as Jerry could run the show. They shook hands without a tentative finger between them. The nine Summit Hill buildings totaling 1168 prime units emerged from the ground in bolts with Wolman's boundless energy.

Summit Hill became an instant success as mostly middle-class Jewish Washingtonian families soon called it home. Not only lauded for its popularity and fast rate of occupancy, Summit Hill is often alluded to when builders and developers discuss a "community" concept with plentiful "green space" gently surrounding the bricks and mortar.

There were several keys to the Summit Hill phenomenon. Being well-located on the borderline between the District and Maryland, with D.C. only a block away, it became the ideally desired residence of choice. The interiors of the modern look apartments were ever so spacious and overwhelmingly well-accented. Moreover, as new renters moved out of their former homes, Summit Hill was the only apartment complex that could provide ample three and four-bedroom suites. The renowned residences suddenly became the rage all over town. Within a year, Summit Hill had rented 700 apartments without ever placing an ad in any newspaper.

In order to insure that even those without the initial funds to afford the deluxe property could rent at Summit Hill, Wolman quietly offered them a magnanimous living arrangement. That year dozens of people knocked on Wolman's trailer in need. One young man had just married and couldn't afford the rent, while another was in between jobs and down on his luck. To those with monetary hardships, Wolman privately proposed that he would allow six months free rent. This gesture stunned its recipients into tears, but when rumors spread of the landlord's acts of kindness, Wolman denied the stories.

But perhaps the most intriguing story was never told. Nearly a year and a half after completion and capacity leasing, Nick Basiliko's wife left him. A depressed Basiliko explained to Jerry that he'd had enough with land grabs and gambles, and wanted to stay at Summit Hill to manage the apartments himself. Nick offered to buy Jerry's half interest for $1,350,000. Jerry downright refused, and peered at Nick with a slow brilliant grin.

"Nick, I cannot charge my partner the same as the market would bring. However, I've never before made a clear $1,000,000 on a deal; so pay me a million and it's yours." Basiliko smiled incredulously. They locked and pumped hands again as before.

Nick asked when they could settle. Jerry replied with a shoulder shrug, "Today." They drove together to the District Title Company. A Deed was drawn and signed in exchange for Nick's signature on a check with six zeroes prefaced by a "1." No lawyers, accountants, bankers, clerks nor clerics were involved when Jerry Wolman split his heralded high rise baby, and strolled down the street with a million dollar Solomon's smile.

# Office Buildings

By the summer of 1959, Jerry Wolman's business dealings were literally growing out of control. However, one morning a young woman came into his life and changed everything. Claire (Farrar) Buete, a petite eighteen-year-old blonde dazzler, had been hired by Jerry's brother Manny as a front desk receptionist for the Company. Jerry arrived for work the next morning to begin his usual sixteen to eighteen hour day and was delighted to glance at such a lovely female behind her desk at the entrance.

"Hey there, Cutie," he gleamed and winked with all the wickedness of his misspent youth, greeting the young initiate while hopping sideways onto her desk.

"Charmed, I'm sure," Claire retaliated coldly while attempting to get her desk organized. Thinking he was the boss's knucklehead son, she cavalierly ignored his childish initiation.

"What's your name?" asked Jerry.

"Claire," she responded barely making eye contact. "What's yours?"

With his resplendent smile aglow and raised eyebrows, he pointed to the Jerry Wolman Construction Company sign on the wall. "Please, call me Jerry." He extended his hand to shake hers, which she reciprocated sheepishly but without a flush.

Over the next weeks, Jerry and Manny noted Claire's mature composure, her even-keel reliability and good-natured contacts with all around her. She had a meticulous knack for keeping tabs on appointments and phone calls needing responses, for scheduling and timing of meetings and for being calmly competent during emergencies. All of these qualities impressed Jerry who was so far over his head in commitments, deadlines and deals that he could hardly think to look at his watch for the correct time. Desperate for Claire's skills, Wolman soon promoted the teenager to become his personal secretary and the Company's bookkeeper. In no time at all, the young blonde belle organized Wolman's entire operation. For thirty years thereafter, Ms. Buete kept a separate longhand ledger budget for each building job and real estate transaction, wrote all Company checks upon receipt of proper vouchers, and maintained the economic structure of Jerry's professional finances as if she were his personal monetary trainer. Under the most difficult circumstances, among brutish contractors, hollering payees and blasphemous bankers, Jerry never heard the wholesome Claire even utter the word, "damn." More importantly, Jerry never realized how little he knew about the detailed financial nitty-gritty of his own business until decades later after Claire had left the company.

*****

By 1961 Jerry Wolman Construction Company included a growing force of three hundred employees and sub-contractors, $50,000 in weekly payroll and over a dozen high rises in Maryland and Virginia. Wolman was steamrolling along the Potomac and churning the waters in barrels of cash.

Growing bolder with each blueprint, his first high-rise intended to scrape the sky, Clear View Towers, contained over 1100 units set apart in three 22-story buildings. At the time, they were the tallest in Montgomery County, Maryland. These concrete structures were spurting out of their foundations at the Wolman pre-set schedule of a floor a week. The financial success of Clear View opened the eyes of real estate financiers and visionary buyers riveted to Wolman's quality and speed of construction. The doors opened for the Company to complete the 12-story Fort Ward Towers, the ten-story Edsel Garden and the 17-story Georgian Towers within a year.

Feeling utterly invincible with each building's triumph, Wolman directed his attention to office buildings, expanding his horizons into the nation's capital. In 1962, he contracted seven successful high rise office towers in a ten block one mile radius within the District of Columbia. The first endeavor was the Executive Building which included 190,000 square feet of office space at 15th and L Street. Wolman had retained the services of Mort Bender and the Blake Construction Company to assist him. However, many cautioned the inexperienced city-developer that Bender had a reputation for wily negotiating and feared that Blake Construction might take advantage of him.

"Morty," Jerry said, "people have warned me not to work with you. If you hurt me, this project will be the only job you'll ever do for me."

After that admonition, Morty Bender could not have been more fair. Surprisingly, most projects came in under budget which led to a succession of successful skyscrapers equaling 1,250,000 square feet of ideal office space. The heart of D.C.'s prime downtown historic district began to beat to the rhythm of Wolman's drum.

His empire now surmounted an equity accumulation of $18,000,000, and the press hailed Jerry Wolman as "The Boy Wonder" of real estate. Ted Dailey's contacts in the Loan Department of the John Hancock Mutual Life Insurance Company were now calling Wolman incessantly to anticipate his upcoming years' projections for funding. Jerry found himself as the Life Insurance Company's largest borrower and its most insured person. Soon he was using his funds to buy buildings of importance in Washington to convert or rehabilitate them into significant high rise office buildings.

*****

Wolman bought The Raleigh Hotel on the northeast corner of Pennsylvania Avenue and 12th Street, NW, a stone's throw from both the White House and the Washington Monument. The Hotel had its start in 1893 when converted from an office building. It had engulfed 12th Street by the addition of floors and at least one major expansion, only to be razed in 1911 for a newer more stylish thirteen-story Beaux Arts edifice facing Pennsylvania Avenue. Jerry saw it as prime office space, as did its original builders. After holding a public auction and the very last of the Tiffany light fixtures had been sold off, The Raleigh Hotel was reduced to rubble once more.

Shortly after receiving the financing, the building permits and placing the construction contracts, Wolman received a telephone call which Claire rapidly reported over their intercom, "It's the White House!"

"Tell 'em I can't do anything about that Berlin Wall," Jerry said, convinced that someone was playing a prank. Claire advised most seriously, "Answer the phone."

Then Jerry heard the unmistakable voice of President John F. Kennedy. "I'd like to meet with you," was all he could remember that JFK said. The young President was Jerry's hero, and the young builder from Shenandoah was absolutely thrilled at the invitation to the White House. Their meeting occurred a few days later and Jerry was startled at the subject matter. Squirming in modest discomfort from a tightly knotted tie, Jerry nervously listened as the President asked him for a favor. Kennedy did not want Jerry to architecturally construct the newly named Federal Building (formerly The Raleigh Hotel) as Wolman had previously planned. JFK expressed concern that to do it would destroy his own plan for the proposed "Beautification of Pennsylvania Avenue." The President asked Wolman to consider redesigning the project by surrendering some fifty feet of the building's footprint and frontage to comply with the President's program. Doing so meant Jerry's having to go back and amend the already approved plans and permits, restructuring the financing and delaying construction. Wolman pondered that the reduced sizing would also reduce his bottom line. In a moment of exceptional public spirit, Jerry's words poured from between his lips as if he were a puzzled but patriotic genie, "Mr. President, your wish is my command."

The President as well as the press lauded Wolman's decision. Citing his example, the Administration called upon developers to follow suit. While others hemmed, hawed and bickered, Wolman remained contritely pleased to have stared Kennedy in the face and reply with what he could do for his country.

# Friends Of The Theatre

In a sensationally dramatic act in early 1963, Jerry Wolman purchased The National Theatre Building and the adjacent Munsey Trust Building on Pennsylvania Avenue for an eye-popping $5,000,000. It was in the National's second floor billiard parlor that John Wilkes Booth is reputed to have stood behind the 8-ball, and at the National's ground floor theatre's box office that Eleanor Roosevelt stood to purchase tickets using dimes from her purse. It was not unnoticed by Shenandoah's high school drop-out that the building he now owned had been visited by every President of the United States since it had opened in 1835. In fact, the boxes on the auditorium's left side had just been enlarged to accommodate the anticipated visits by John Kennedy's rather large extended family. The chance to be so intimate with history thrilled Wolman.

The Munsey Trust Building on the National's left had been built as the Imperial Hotel at the turn of the 20th century, and had later housed the *Washington Post* and The Munsey Trust. The venerable Trust's lease was about to expire and needed renewal when Jerry decided to buy both legendary buildings. Wolman recalled in the back of his mind that in the mid-1950's Munsey Trust had turned him down coldly for a small loan, viewing him as having far too meager a financial statement. Joking with the straightest face but with amused inner laughter, Jerry returned the favor. Before he renewed its lease within the building he now owned, he required a detailed substantiation of the Trust's assets. After a brief minute of karmic satisfaction and levity, the lease was extended and the deal made complete.

Grand inaugural parades and important demonstrations marched up and down Pennsylvania Avenue past the two buildings. Wolman was pleased as Punch to parlay a long-term lease for the penthouse floor of his nearby (Raleigh Hotel) Federal Building to the FBI. The Bureau's marksmen and lookouts maneuvered placement of agents throughout the office building's top windows at such festivities to protect against any untoward events among the crowds along the Avenue.

Jerry had purchased a panorama of American perspectives with his friends and partners Stanley Reines, Sidney Teplin, Ed Dreyfuss, Stanley Rosensweig and Frank Luchs. Wolman brought them along to enjoy the view with him. The partners' equitable agreements were reached in the spirit of Wolman's noteworthy overall view of entrepreneurial ethics. Those lucky enough to call Jerry Wolman their friend received opportunities to prosper like no others. Jerry got the men the elaborate financing needed so that none of them had to spare a dime.

Wolman genuinely loved people and placed tremendous value on his friendships. From as far back as his childhood "Shendo" days, Jerry considered his close contemporaries as if they were his own blood. Years later, Jerry never felt more fortunate than when he was able to help his friends establish themselves in business. His reward was immeasurable as he watched with energetic empathy the expressions on the faces of others who were succeeding. Rarely seen in business, even if a competitor needed help, Jerry would not flinch. His theory assumed that the proverbial pie was big enough to go around.

\*\*\*\*\*

Back in the late 1950's, one of the first to approach Jerry was Sidney Teplin. The two had met and become amicable nearly a decade earlier. Teplin's father was in the "shmata business" dealing in the trading of a multitude of brick-a-brack items in a hole-in-the-wall store a block from Mr. Ackerholt's Colonial Wallpaper. There young Sidney had started a small check-cashing enterprise while attending accounting school in the evenings. Jerry frequented the store each week to get cash for Ackerholt's register. The two spoke and yearned of breaking away.

Years later, when words of Jerry's meteoric career shouted from newspaper headlines, Teplin, a maturing accounting school graduate, approached Wolman seeking advice on starting his own construction business. At the same time, Jerry's neighbor and card-carrying poker player, Stanley Reines, appeared at Jerry's front door for similar mentoring. Wolman believed Stanley was handy enough and had the ability to learn the building trade, and that Sidney was adept with figures and had street smarts. He introduced the two to partner. Neither Teplin nor Reines had the slightest idea where to start, nor did either have the funding to begin. But Wolman saw the opportunity for them and knew that it would be good.

Jerry worked by their side to locate a piece of property to his liking. He kept Sid and Stan nearby when he visited with the architect, the engineer, the contractors and the lender's administrative staffers. Wolman then fronted the money needed to obtain initial financing and signed guarantees of loans for construction and permanent lending. The great Samaritan then spent days on the project to make sure that Sundial Apartments in Suitland, Maryland was successful for his friends. It was, and the sun shined brightly on Stan's and Sid's fortunes. Jerry had no financial nor other interest in the garden apartment project, except the pleasure of being able to help. He felt as if he were paying back the powers-that-be for having been so good to him.

Sidney and Stanley became hugely successful builders and partnered with Jerry on the National Theatre/Munsey Trust transaction where only Jerry fronted and guaranteed the funding, taking all the risks upon his shoulders alone.

On a tender note, the pie was even larger and sweeter than anyone could have anticipated. Sidney Teplin fell in love with Jerry's sister Sandy who, after her predicted fortune-told divorce, fell in love with Sid, and married.

*****

Wolman started many in businesses and personally guided them through fruition. One afternoon in 1962, Marty Weil came home early from work and hollered up the steps of his small home in Silver Spring, Maryland for his wife Dorothy. She was surprised by his arrival and walked down to meet him. Dorothy was greeted by five words that changed her life.

"I'm quitting the kitchen business!" her husband declared. Marty, a young flourishing Vice President of the kitchen division at Zamoski and Co. stood before his wife excitedly.

"Are you crazy?" she responded. Marty was making $125 per week, and Dorothy thought they were living high on the hog.

"Jerry Wolman's going to teach me the building business," he said absolutely with no fear of failure. "I'm going to be a builder!"

Blown away, Dorothy sat down at the kitchen table with sudden interest. Notwithstanding, her rational side soon intervened.

"That sounds great," she said cautiously, still shocked in disbelief, "but in the meantime, how are we gonna live?"

Marty reached into his pocket, took out a check and slammed it on the table in front of her. The check totaled $5,000 and was signed by Jerry Wolman.

"This should tide us over for groceries," he gloated.

Successful future builders such as Ziggy Chelec, Jan Strompf, Harry Rosen, Alan Kay, Buddy Rozansky, Stanley Bobb, Jerry Schiff, Jack Buete and so many others too numerous to name, all received their bountiful first ride on Jerry's train. They held Wolman in awe for fronting their projects, guarantying their loans and personally grinding a smooth path for their livelihoods. They expressed their appreciation and gratitude in a plethora of ways, but in truth, the real joy was Jerry's.

As word hit the streets that Wolman was accumulating apprentices in the building business, young men appeared for jobs on Jerry's sites. They had been sent by their mothers, to learn from and become a "Jerry Wolman." He turned no one away, and gave each to Frank Bolek for suitable training and work. The joke on the job was to see how long the darlings would last. To start they dug ditches, carried heavy lumber, hauled bricks and hammered long nails into seasoned wood. Aching from every limb, most did not return the following day. Those that survived a week were earmarked for promotion to begin the climb up the ladder of Wolman's enterprises.

# A Childhood Dream

Jerry Wolman's prodigious real estate beanstalk had surpassed all clouds in the skies over Washington and was booming upward through giant monthly deals. Each transaction gave birth to a golden egg. Prices of realty were being goosed so perfectly by the growing economy that his investments soared in value. Unafraid of risk, and with instinctive acumen for acreage, Jerry was signing contracts for tracts that he then sold at 100% profit within months. He also maintained and directed almost a dozen building projects, juggling them deftly with his team in harness.

After eight years of rolling momentum, he was responsible for the construction of approximately thirty thousand apartment units and almost eight million square feet of office space. The $18,000,000 in available personal equity with which he'd begun 1962 was nearing $36,000,000 just eighteen months later. And he wasn't stopping there. Nearly a month after the National Theatre, Wolman purchased the Annapolis Roads Country Club and thereafter ventured into developing shopping centers. Mentally invincible, it seemed to him there was nothing that he couldn't have or couldn't do.

By 1963, Wolman had become somewhat of a likeably cocky local celebrity. He became a "regular" at Duke Zeibert's Connecticut Avenue restaurant, devouring steaks and lobsters with his table-sharing shamans: sports columnist Shirley Povich, radio-gabber Larry King and brilliant D.C. attorney Edward Bennett Williams. Never to be outdone, and wealthy beyond wisdom, Wolman began to genuinely enjoy his ascent.

Being overtly and ostentatiously excessive was now within Jerry's realm. Eating at Duke Zeibert's long forty-foot table, Wolman was seated at the head of an entourage of thirty of his guests dining along each side of him. Buddy Rozansky was the thirty-first at the other end of the table facing Jerry and drinking in merriment. Reveling in the largeness of his party and livelihood, Jerry, feigning business, had a phone brought to him. Cupping his hands over the receiver, he whispered to the operator to contact Western Union located a few doors away, and continued on the line.

Ten minutes later, a young gentleman dressed in cap and uniform rushed to the center of the restaurant and called out imperatively, "Telegram for Mr. Rozansky. Urgent telegram for Mr. Bud Rozansky!" He exuberantly announced its critical arrival to the room.

Rozansky seemed frozen as he stood up and motioned for the guided paper missile. All tablemates turned silent as the restaurant held its collective breath with intrigue. Buddy's complexion turned burgundy as he opened the Western Union envelope. He burst his shirt-buttons laughing as he read the message out loud with raging relief: "Could you pass me the salt? – Jerry."

*****

Celebrated Washington sports writer, "Mo" Siegel, was a nightly fixture at Duke Zeibert's. Dining at Duke's with such regularity, he used to say he was "eating out" whenever his wife cooked for him at home. Jerry adored the sports stories and background banter that the *Washington Star* and *Washington Post* columnist delivered every evening over dinner. Mo chatted unilaterally each night about sports to anyone willing to nod in agreement. The sports-fan-builder and the famed journalist became sociable cohorts. Siegel had often laughed loudly about and even choked over Wolman's overabundant adoration of his childhood team, the Philadelphia Eagles.

One particular twilight night, with a glowing sunset in the clouded skies, Jerry arrived at Duke's to see Mo seated behind a cleared table waiting for him. He beckoned Jerry to the plush corner of the room where he always sat, and pointed an index finger at the seat directly next to him.

"Have I got news for you," he intoned in a low grumble, looking around to protect his secret. Curious, Wolman sat down.

"This is strictly confidential, but my sources tell me it's true blue," he stated quietly as he leaned into Jerry's face. "I heard the Eagles are for sale," Siegel exhaled. Mo straightened the napkin on his lap and for the first time nodded at someone else in the room.

Wolman was hit by a demonstrative bolt of lightning. His lower jaw dropped two full inches and his eyes glazed toward his future. Jerry knew instantly that if there were any way whatsoever to purchase his beloved team, he'd take every viable action in his power. He thanked Mo and left Duke's precipitously without eating a thing.

That night Jerry couldn't sleep a wink. All he could envision was the dream he'd had since he was a child. Back then, football was his only release from the long arduous hours of labor. Unable to play for his high school team due to his responsibilities in the family business, a large aching void still remained in his soul. Restlessly, he thought of his dear football friend Johnny Robel and their one hundred mile ticket-less hikes to Eagles home games. Back then, he eventually knew the security guard who let him in at the "halftime gate." Now, twenty years later and two hundred miles away, he did not know a soul to help him find an Eagles' entrance.

Jerry drove from Washington D.C. to Philadelphia the next morning, straight to the Old Original Bookbinder's seafood restaurant at Second and Walnut Streets. Wolman had taken a few business trips to look at a number of properties in Philadelphia in the late 1950's. He frequented the establishment and recalled that most of the city's movers and shakers dined there. Jerry was mesmerized by the autographed pictures of the movie stars and sports figures which adorned the walls. The celebrities' arms were always entangled in embraces with those of the owner. Jerry sensed that the owner might be able to shed some light on the Eagles' nest. Taking a deep breath, Wolman anxiously entered the legendary establishment and walked around.

"Can I help you?" asked the bartender. Lost in the wall's pictures, Wolman ignored him. "Sir, is there anything I can help you with?" the bartender questioned again.

"Oh I'm sorry," Jerry returned from his spell. "Actually, I'd like to speak with the owner."

John Taxin, the sage and beneficent owner of Bookbinder's approached Jerry, his unannounced first customer of the day. Wolman realized that he wasn't quite sure what he was going to say to the man despite a four hour car ride in which to prepare. After a brief introduction and some chatter regarding a few of the sports figures on the wall, Jerry attempted to tell Mr. Taxin his ambitious intentions. Taxin quickly learned of Wolman's reputation in real estate, but was more impressed by the vibrant, honest, handsome and gutsy businessman. They spoke for three contagiously friendly hours in the side barroom reserved for VIP's. Wolman shared with Taxin that years ago on many late-night drives to Philadelphia as a young teen loading his produce truck at Dock Street, Jerry remembered seeing a string of lavish limousines outside the restaurant's alley. Taxin warmed to Jerry when the builder revealed that he always wished he had stepped inside. Each liked the other very much, and in seeing Wolman's obvious charismatic passion, Taxin agreed to help him.

"It's going to be a long shot, but I'll do what I can to see that you get a real chance at purchasing the team." In the same breath, John Taxin warned Jerry of the political affiliations and politicians' games that are played at times in the city of "Brotherly Shove."

"Let's see if we can get the right people and steer you in the right direction," Taxin concluded.

＊＊＊＊＊

The first thing Wolman learned was that the Eagles club was owned by a group of sixty-five prominent local stockholders, and was effectively led by the Commissioner of Philadelphia's Fire Department, Frank McNamee. Mr. Taxin had prepared Jerry for McNamee, an old tough customer and a renowned straight shooter. After calling him a couple of times from Washington without making contact, Wolman finally succeeded in making an appointment after revealing his reason. McNamee sounded as gruff as a fire truck engine, but allowed for a visit in his station's office. Jerry appeared on time, richly dressed in his best suit. At the meeting, the gritty

Commissioner gave Wolman a rough time, and sanctioned the wealthy builder that he was neither impressed by his youth nor the silver spoon in his mouth with which he was obviously born. Not wanting to debate McNamee's assessment, Jerry held fast respectfully and said, "Commissioner, sooner or later when the facts come out, I think you'll see that I'm a bit older than I look and that our backgrounds are not dissimilar." The Commissioner fired many questions at Jerry and seemed unimpressed by his lack of experience. Branded an outsider, Jerry felt as if he were spiraling down a fire pole leading to absolutely nowhere.

As Wolman was escorted out by the Commissioner, they passed a well-worn pool table in the center of the firehouse.

"Youngsters wouldn't know anything about an old-timer's game like billiards," McNamee sneered at Jerry.

"Well," replied Wolman in nascent hustler's naiveté, "I know a *little* bit about it. May I?"

A whistling Wolman went for a cue stick and placed the 8-ball in the center of the green felt at one edge of the table. Then he set a cue ball on the very opposite end of the table directly in line with it. Still acting as if he almost knew what he was doing, Jerry applied a dash of chalk to the end of his stick, lined it up, and called the shot in the right hand pocket: a near impossible angle. Wolman looked at McNamee with a flagrant grin, and then hit the cue ball, striking the 8-ball directly into the aforementioned right corner pocket as if it had eyes. With enough English, the cue ball bounced off three walls and came right back to the exact spot from which it had been struck. McNamee let out a cackling roar and respectfully whacked Wolman playfully on his back. Secretly, Jerry was even more surprised. Truth be told, even Henny Kibuilis' pals at the pool halls of Shenandoah would have been proud of that fated click of the stick.

The ice was broken between the Fire Commissioner and the wealthy upstart. The auspicious pool shot did more for Jerry's chances at acquiring the Eagles than his entire construction history. McNamee glad-handed Jerry good-bye, "Come back next week and we'll talk some more."

# THE FAVOR

Earl Foreman, Wolman's closest confidant and astute attorney, introduced his wife Phyllis and her immediate relatives to Jerry back in the mid-1950's. At family gatherings, Wolman met Phyllis' stout father Sol Snider, along with her brother Ed, a bright young recent graduate from the University of Maryland. Jerry took an instant liking to Sol who was also involved in the real estate business and more than a dozen years wiser. Wolman revered and looked up to him. Over the years, the two met for business meetings at San Souci's restaurant downtown to discuss a few deals, eat and enjoy each other's company.

In 1962 Sol informed Jerry of his interest in founding the Public National Bank, and convinced Jerry to invest. Wolman did, and later began to use the bank as his own depository and promoted others, including the owner of San Souci's, to do so. Jerry had nothing but the highest admiration for Sol Snider, a well-respected, first-class and honest businessman whom he considered a good friend.

Jerry had not been following Ed Snider's career closely. He had heard that Eddie, six years his junior, and a co-partner Gerald Lillienfield were involved in the record business. One day in early 1962, Ed, now twenty-seven, called Jerry to ask him for a favor. Snider was short payroll for his record company Edge Limited, and needed a small $4,000 to $5,000 loan. Jerry replied with his usual "sure," and did so. Ed and Gerald repaid him promptly in due course the following week. This initial interest-free loan started a precedent of calls from Ed and Gerald once or twice a month in dire need of short-term funds. Each time, even though the loans sometimes ballooned to $10,000, Jerry assented. By April of 1962, Lillienfield grew tired of borrowing with no visible profits in sight, and sold out of the company to his partner Eddie. For many months thereafter, Jerry loaned additional sums almost every other week. Then Edge Limited and Ed Snider suddenly had difficulty paying Wolman back. The record company's debts to Jerry quickly totaled in the range of $30,000. Wolman was flush and sorry for a young go-getter like Ed, and out of loyalty to Sol Snider and Earl Foreman, raised little if any fuss.

Eventually, Ed called Jerry to explain that he would be unable to repay him and asked Wolman if he'd consider taking stock in the record company in lieu of the cash he owed. Jerry responded with his usual answer to the son of a long-time friend, "No problem." Wolman received the all-but-worthless stock and forgave the young man's loans. A few months thereafter by the end of 1962, Snider's Edge Limited business went broke and closed, belly up.

Soon Snider came to Wolman with the opportunity to sell the remnants of his company to Pioneer Airlines. Pioneer could make use of Edge's losses on its books for a tax benefit. Ed needed Jerry on board for the Pioneer deal to take off, and Jerry agreed to transfer his stock for little more than airline peanuts. Although disappointed by his losses, Wolman was impressed by Snider's tenacity and shrewd maneuvering to commandeer the sale, barely landing on his feet.

Shortly thereafter in the summer of 1963, Ed seemed discontented over his failed business, and began his search to find his next endeavor. One afternoon a distraught Sol Snider telephoned his friend Jerry. His voice trembling, Sol was helpless with concern over his son's troubled state. Fearing for his only son's well-being, Sol pleaded for Jerry to intervene.

"Jerry, I'm worried about Eddie," said his father fretfully. "He's just not himself," Sol stuttered, "he's very depressed."

Wolman listened soberly and attempted to settle Sol Snider down.

Sol interrupted, "If there's anything you can do to help him Jerry, I would consider it a tremendous favor."

After having started so many in businesses and helped countless others get jobs, Wolman understood clearly what Sol was asking of him. Jerry assured Sol that he would meet with Ed immediately, and made a promise to his close friend to do whatever he could to help him. Sol arranged for Jerry to pick up Eddie in 45 minutes at 16th and K Street in Washington, just down the block from Sol's bank office. When Wolman saw the young Snider standing on the street corner, he realized that there were serious problems indeed. Ed looked like a multi-day unshaven, disheveled vagabond. Pulling over to the curb, Jerry was suddenly as concerned as Eddie's father.

Snider plopped into the car sullen and downtrodden in demeanor. Jerry tried to cheer him up, but nothing at all seemed to work. In a moment of unabashed empathy, Jerry confided in strictest secrecy that he was negotiating on an endeavor to bid on the Philadelphia Eagles football franchise. Before Wolman could even complete his sentence, an instantaneous change came over Ed. Snider sat up straight, eagerly wanting to know the specifics about the prospects and plans. Wolman observed Snider's impressive transformation and overwhelming interest, and further promised Ed he'd make room for him somewhere if the purchase came to fruition. Snider's vagrant-bearded chin lifted with hope and he smiled spiritedly at Jerry. Wolman told him to sit tight and that he'd be kept in the loop as matters progressed. Ed could barely contain himself with enthusiasm and gratitude as Jerry drove him back to his father's office a new man.

Sol Snider called Jerry that night to thank him profusely and to say he'd never forget the favor. Jerry reiterated his promise to help Eddie in honor of Sol's friendship over the years. That night Wolman thought to himself that if it weren't the Eagles, he'd do something else to keep his word to Sol.

# The Bid

A complete outsider, Wolman knew no one well enough nor trusted hardly a soul in Philadelphia.

"The shareholders are a close-knit group who do favors and look out for each other," Taxin warned. "Just be careful," he said, "you don't know who's on whose side."

John Taxin seemed the only person Wolman could count on, and maintaining discretion was vital in a bidding process which Jerry suspiciously feared was extremely political and forbidding. Through Taxin, Jerry was able to capture a wide angle photograph of the Eagles' financial picture. The club had sixty-five shareholders owning a total of ninety-one shares. Within Bookbinders' walls, some insiders and talkative stockholders revealed to Taxin that they'd be pleased if each share of stock were bid in to bring $60,000 a piece. Therefore, a total sealed bid of $5,460,000 (91 shares x $60,000), he suggested, would surely be the top winning bid. Wolman, however, had concerns that everyone to whom he spoke was calculating.

Taxin advised Jerry to use a politically savvy former state senator Harry Shapiro, Esq. as his counsel. Shapiro had been elected to represent a goodly portion of Philadelphia in the Pennsylvania state senate as a Republican in 1932. As the New Deal came to fruition under FDR, Harry changed his horse's color and registered as a Democrat, to be elected to two more terms. In 1954, with support from both sides of the aisle, Shapiro was appointed Pennsylvania's Secretary of Welfare. His public career had made him powerful allies in the Pennsylvania Legislature, especially in its investigating committees, and when he returned to private practice in Philadelphia there was no doubt that his connections were impeccable. By 1963 Harry Shapiro was nearing three-quarters of a century on earth, with almost half that time having grown accustomed to the dirtiest of his city's political encounters. Harry was sharp, jovial and polished. An uncomplicated and straightforward attorney, Shapiro once told Jerry, "If you can't do an Agreement on two sheets of paper, it's not worth the paper it's written on." That philosophy squared with Wolman's values, although Jerry preferred to make sure that the backsides of each sheet were blank.

The lawyer and his client met fifteen times in Shapiro's downtown Philadelphia brownstone offices and painstakingly reviewed the past three years of Eagles' books and records. They examined all of the team's assets and liabilities, debts, players' salaries and all other contracts of significance. Jerry scanned the maze of math to the penny. He figured that when all was said and done with his plans, Wolman's Eagles would *lose* $250,000 per year. Shapiro stepped away and closely observed Wolman's reaction.

"Not much of an investment," Harry blurted.

"Are you kidding?" countered Jerry. "This is an investment in *happiness*, short and long term."

Wolman wanted to make certain his counsel understood that this was the culmination of a longtime dream and he'd let nothing get in its way of coming true. Before leaving that afternoon, Jerry swore everyone in Shapiro's practice to utmost secrecy. Wolman's determined attitude to acquire the Eagles had manifested itself into near obsession over the next month.

In their final meeting, Shapiro and Wolman carefully considered that the team's shareholders had originally set an initial sale price of $4,500,000, an unheard of sum for a non-producing profitless enterprise. Thereafter the shareholders preferred a sealed bid process, hoping to foster an even higher price through competition. Jerry and Harry huddled and determined they would submit a bid of $5,305,000 in a sealed envelope on December 5th, 1963. The bid contract was typed on two pages of paper alluding to that sum in its contents, placed in Shapiro's envelope and locked in his briefcase.

The surfacing competition was fierce, including Philadelphia's entrenched magnate businessman Jack Wolgin, the apparent front runner, and Jack McCrane, son-in-law of Eugene Mori, owner of the Garden State Race Track. Each of them had a battery of high-powered lawyers working on their respective bids and appeared reservedly optimistic.

In the days leading up to the bidding, Wolman became wary of everyone, unsure he could trust even his own counsel, Harry Shapiro. When the day arrived, Jerry walked north six blocks alongside Harry from the lawyer's office to Broad Street's Fidelity Building with a lump in his throat. His concentration on anything other than being the owner of the Philadelphia Eagles had disappeared from cognition. Unbeknownst to anyone, Wolman had his secretary Claire Buete type an exact replica of the bid the day before. However, he had changed the monetary figure upward to $5,505,500.

Nearly a few blocks from the entrance of the building, Jerry asked Harry for one last look at the bid. Shapiro curiously retrieved the envelope from his briefcase and handed it to him. Then Jerry replaced Shapiro's papers with what had been typed by Claire, and returned it to his lawyer.

"You're raising the bid?" muttered Shapiro incredulously. The attorney studied the number meticulously and shook his head. "It's too high."

"Senator, maybe it is, but I want this club so badly," stated Wolman passionately. "I just can't take the chance of losing it."

The two respectfully disagreed for a few minutes, but in the end his counsel agreed. Shapiro took the new papers and re-deposited them into the envelope. Now both men were on the same two pages.

At 4:00 p.m., only attorneys and shareholders were allowed into the huge conference room. The room was furnished with spindle-backed captain's chairs surrounding a long walnut table shined to accommodate the importance of the event. Jerry waited anxiously alone outside the thick wooden doors, apart from all other bidders, members of the press and Eagle enthusiasts.

Muffled sounds snuck from under the closed doors as the bids were opened by McNamee and announced. Jerry's high bid brought uproar, with yells of "Default!" and "Objection!" One attorney's voice stood out and decried, "I motion we postpone the bidding, we need more time!" There was unexpected mayhem inside the room and confusion whirled outside of it. Sitting apart helplessly, Wolman closed his eyes, then hoped, wished and prayed.

Harry Shapiro's shouting was heard above all guttural utterances, "I'll sue everybody in this room!" Over the ruckus, McNamee banged the table to a hush. With the opinion of the room chaotically divided for almost four heated hours, the influential Fire Commissioner finally stood, holding everyone's attention with the weight of his authority. The man who had at first disliked Jerry calmly announced that all sealed bids had been opened and announced according to the rules and the law.

"Mr. Wolman's bid was in conformity, and the highest," reminded the Commissioner, and took matters to a tension-filled vote for approval. After the shareholders' votes had been counted, fifty of the ninety-one available shares narrowly elected to sell the franchise to Wolman.

"Jerry Wolman is the owner of the Philadelphia Eagles," McNamee declared, "Good day!"

Through the long wait, Jerry had no idea what had happened, nor did the masses who were packing the anteroom. Suddenly the doors to the conference room flew open and Harry Shapiro wriggled through the crowd toward Wolman.

"We won!" Shapiro exclaimed, his voice rising again, his fists clenched. As the two men shook hands triumphantly, lights from blinding flashbulbs careened into Jerry's dilating eyes.

An impromptu press conference emerged from the raucousness. Jerry found himself behind a microphone and podium fielding questions. His tie had opened as he cavalierly smoked a cigarette. The reporters continued to blazon his face with flashing bulbs, pumping him with inquiries. Wolman was light-hearted, proud and as jocular as a juvenile. Jerry had suddenly become the youngest owner in the National Football League. Noting that at thirty-six years of age Jerry had amassed $36,000,000, one columnist coyly asked the new owner, "How does a man make a million dollars for every year of his life?"

Wolman's laugh was contagious, "I don't know exactly," he

modestly responded shaking his head. Then after taking a drag of his cigarette he smiled, "but I can't wait 'til I'm fifty!"

Television reporters and members of the media clamored for background on the little-known builder from Washington. Journalists from the *Evening Bulletin*, the *Inquirer* and the *Daily News* scrambled to payphones in the Fidelity lobby to call in the story, still thrilled by a breath of fresh air that had blown into their news. Wolman owned the Eagles and the press.

Jerry eventually learned that he could have lost the bidding had he not switched to the higher figure prior to entering the building. His intuition had played a perfect shot.

One of Philadelphia's finest, Bill Fishman, the President of ARA Services' large and growing food concession company, came up to Jerry to congratulate him.

"Are you going back to D.C. tonight?" Bill asked. Jerry wanted badly to catch a flight that night to tell his wife Anne in person what had happened.

"Let me help," insisted Fishman, whose limousine drove Wolman to the ARA private jet. Jerry flew off as soon as clearance was given and landed in Washington after midnight that evening. There, another limo was waiting for him supplied by the Fishman family, and Jerry was jockeyed home.

He wanted nothing more than to surprise Anne in his arms with the greatest news of their lives. She was unaware of the afternoon's events, and not having heard from her husband, decided to go to sleep. Jerry marched carefully up the bottom steps to his bedroom in a darkened house. Excited, though nearly exhausted, he called upstairs to his dozing wife, "Anne, you won't believe what happened!" The Eagles, the press conference, the cheers and the private jet were all on the tip of his eager tongue. His drowsy wife managed the following phrase from her pillow, "Tell me everything, honey, right after you take out the garbage."

# Closing Down The Bar

For as long as Jerry could remember, there were two things which seemed to meld together: Football and Johnny Robel. From the time they were children, they shared dreams of one day having their own football team.

After serving as a Navy quartermaster aboard the cruiser USS Atlanta in the Philippines and Okinawa campaigns of World War II, John Robel muscled his way into restaurant and night club businesses. He married his beautiful hometown Shendo sweetheart "Willie," and spent twelve years working at "The Patio" in Palm Beach, Florida, migrating in the off-seasons to toil at a country club in Levittown, New Jersey. Johnny then became the banquet manager at the Barclay Hotel in Philadelphia for five years before he and Willie moved back home to Shenandoah to operate as proprietors of their own bar/restaurant: *"Johnny Robel's."*

"Johnny Robel's" was a rather large taproom and eatery on South Main Street with a massive circular bar at its center surrounded by dining tables. Johnny, Willie and their three kids lived happily upstairs, except that the youngsters' received little sound sleep; an undoubted result of the bar's 2:00 a.m. "last call" before closing.

Just days after Jerry's successful adventure at bidding, the entire Philadelphia media thirsted and starved for Wolman. Ironically, Jerry had disappeared to resurface at a bar and restaurant one hundred miles away in his hometown. Unannounced at 9:30 at night, the doors to Robel's establishment swung open ferociously and with purpose. Robel had just bent down to grab a bottle of beer before standing up, his back to the main entrance. Jerry easily recognized Johnny's colossal head and hefty shoulders. Wolman cocked his arm and threw an official NFL football which spiraled across the room, striking his old friend as if there were a painted bull's-eye on the middle of his back. Startled, Robel reacted with a rush of angry adrenalin to throw the reckless heaver out. Johnny turned furiously around only to see the new owner of the Philadelphia Eagles standing there beaming.

"You're outta here," Jerry insisted, "you're coming with me."

Robel stared with sheer disbelief while rubbing his back.

Jerry then approached him, leaned over the bar and started breaking beer glasses one by one onto the floor.

"Hey, are you crazy?" Robel whined. "Knock it off, willya!?"

Anne Wolman entered the restaurant with Arnold Stark, a friend Jerry had hired that afternoon in similar fashion to run the team's Public Relations department.

"We've got the Eagles, John," Wolman postured in regal fashion, "The *Eagles*!...I can't do it without you."

Robel thought to himself gazing around at the business he had built over the past two years. He quickly glanced upstairs where his family was readying for bed and finally back at his oldest friend. Jerry picked up one more glass, held it with two fingers in the air and readied to release it to the ground. The patrons elbowing the bar all watched in silence.

"Sorry folks," Robel apologized to his customers. Nursing a pregnant pause, he announced, "After tonight, we're closed for business!" Johnny broke into the broadest smile looking at Jerry as if twenty years had vanished.

"Then drinks are on me!" Wolman raised hell slapping the bar. People cheered with glee as word scurried about of wild shenanigans at Robel's. Lovingly, Anne went over to embrace Jerry along with Johnny, as Willie Robel came downstairs to check upon the boisterous commotion. Willie nearly fainted at the news they were moving to Philadelphia and joining the professional ranks. Soon the place was packed with people enjoying Jerry's alcoholic guarantee. Robel took Wolman to the side and put his thick forearm around Jerry's neck.

"What will I do?" Johnny asked.

After Jerry rattled off a number of personnel positions, Robel abruptly chose "Equipment Manager." At that moment, John Robel had become the highest paid Equipment Manager in the National Football League. In fact, he was paid more than most coaches. On that memorable and momentous evening, folks simply lost track of the time and the bar remained open well after 2:00 a.m. Then "Johnny Robel's" closed, permanently.

*****

The sun looked even brighter the next day. Occasional clouds passed overhead in shapes like footballs. Or so it seemed to Wolman. One nebulous cloud remained: The vote of the NFL teams' owners for league approval. Eleven of the thirteen owners had to approve him, or the entire escapade would have been for naught.

Jerry initiated an appointment to meet the following week with the National Football League's razor sharp Commissioner, Pete Rozelle. Jerry arrived two hours early with a stomach speaking in languages he'd never heard before or since. A froth of sweat lined his forehead. Jerry fanned himself with a magazine in the outer lobby to cool his nerves and to get some blood flowing in the direction of his head.

Rozelle welcomed Jerry warmly and offered him congratulations with gentlemanly hospitality.

"Jerry," the Commissioner enunciated with eyebrows rising, "we're going to check you out nine ways to Sunday. If you deserve to get in, you'll get in. If you don't deserve to get in, no one or nothing will help you."

An unnerved Jerry nodded at Rozelle. "Commissioner, what happens if you check me out and you think I should get in, but the *owners* turn me down?"

Rozelle stood up and pointed his finger firmly in Jerry's face. "If *anyone* gives you a hard time for an invalid or ill-intended reason, then you and I will fight them together."

Both Wolman and Rozelle knew that some of the league's owners previously had contact with those who'd wanted to purchase the Eagles. Rozelle therefore spoke simply and to the point. Jerry was reassured knowing that his reputation personally and as a businessman could be searched from here to kingdom-come without a problem or reservation.

The Commissioner suggested that Jerry schedule to meet with the other owners to humbly and cordially solicit their approval. The first on Wolman's list to call upon was Art Rooney who presided over the neighboring Pittsburgh Steelers. Jerry called Rooney to ask if he could meet with him in person to discuss an important matter. Over the phone Art instantly invited Jerry to his 63rd birthday party in Pittsburgh that weekend at the "Saints & Sinners" Club.

Wolman was honored to be at the party, and Art Rooney personally introduced Jerry to every important businessman and politician at the affair. At the end of the evening, Rooney approached him in private and asked Jerry what it was he had wished to discuss.

"Commissioner Rozelle thought it would be a good idea," Jerry fumbled, "if I met with some of the owners before the vote on whether or not to approve me."

Art began laughing. "You came all the way to Pittsburgh for that? You know if they checked people out when I was made owner, I'd have never gotten in the league!" Shaking his head, Rooney licked some cake icing off his forefinger and pulled Jerry to his wall phone. Art immediately dialed George Halas of the Bears.

"Listen George, I've got this Wolman fellow here," Rooney cajoled. "Don't make this kid come all the way out to Chicago. He's okay!"

After Rozelle's investigators spotlighted Jerry's honesty, integrity and generous ways, favorable references resulted across the board. With the blessing and backing of the Commissioner, Steelers owner Rooney and Bears owner Halas, Jerry Wolman was approved in the first league meeting unanimously: 13-0.

# Eagles Office – First Day

While Wolman was awaiting the results of the interminable stockholders' meeting outside the fifth floor Fidelity conference room by himself, he was painfully reminded that good fortune and success cannot be truly enjoyed and realized alone. That day of the bidding, Jerry kept in touch every half hour on the phone with his full-time Washington attorney and side-kick, Earl Foreman. When things looked "iffy" and events seemed to be dragging, Jerry called Earl to fly to Philadelphia and wait close by at the Bellevue Stratford Hotel. Wolman considered Foreman a member of his family, as close to a brother as another could have. For years Earl had participated in Jerry's real estate dealings as a gratuitous silent partner. While Foreman never had to put up a dime, Wolman continued to reward his friend and lawyer with a gifted percentage in his dealings everywhere. Riding a tidal wave of money and success lead Wolman to believe that purchasing the Eagles could be his most bodacious gesture to date.

Jerry's human fabric was sewn so that his biggest deal and dream had to be interwoven benevolently with freely given stitches to those working for and with him. He regarded the Philadelphia Eagles as a "family enterprise," and had already devised a plan to include his closest friends. While Jerry maintained the necessary majority ownership of the team, he chose to apportion minority interests to those whom he considered kindred. In a meeting prior to the bidding, Jerry and Earl had discussed Wolman's desire to divvy up individual smaller stakes in the team. Therefore Foreman was to

84

be named with 48% of the football franchise, a minority ownership to be dispersed as options which would eventually be divided by Jerry among his family, friends and employees. For the moment NFL rules made it expedient to simply name Foreman with the full minority interest.

Jerry and Earl met at the Bellevue for a short victory dance after the voting, with raised clasped hands held high in victory. The trust between them was thick and visible, and all that remained to be seen was the beginning of a prosperous and successful football franchise.

*****

Settlement was held on February 4th, 1964, as Jerry gladly handed over his Morgan Guaranty and Trust check of $5,505,000 (plus $500 in cash) and made matters official. The hapless, last place, 2-12, 1963 Eagles now had an owner who resembled a knight in shining armor. The city was abuzz with electrifying hopes for change. Jerry had already won the hearts of the media by displaying his humor and candid ways, and by an unprecedented assurance of an "open door/nothing off the record" policy. Hugh Brown, sportswriter for the *Philadelphia Bulletin* publicly salivated in his column over the impending "clean sweep of the entire Eagles' organization." Jerry sat in his car shaking his head reading Brown's article concerning its call for abundant looming changes in cold pitiless words not spared for the Eagles' staff. Wolman rolled up the newspaper and stepped inside the shabby Locust Street offices of the Eagles brass.

Inside, the mood was despondent as most employees feared that Jerry's first day on the job would also be their last. The place looked like a dilapidated warehouse where each person in the office had gone to work that day to clear his or her belongings for boxed storage. No one made eye contact with the novice owner as Jerry meandered mercifully around sprinkling greetings and pleasantries.

Joe "Jiggs" Donahue had arrived on the administrative staff of the Eagles in 1949. He became the club's Executive Vice President reporting directly to Frank McNamee. At sixty-eight, he'd weathered many storms, but saw through every difficulty with Irish innate good

85

sense. Jerry respectfully approached Donahue's office to speak with him in private. Donahue seemed frightened at Jerry's entry. Jiggs was certain that his fifteen year tenure was about to be truncated by the brash millionaire owner. At Jiggs' age, there was nowhere else to go. To placate him immediately, Jerry spoke softly as if to a treasured companion.

"Mr. Donahue," Wolman said, "regardless of what you may have heard, you're not losing your job. In fact, you're getting a raise."

Donahue's eyes crossed involuntarily, and then opened wide.

"I promise you, sir, you'll have a job here with me for the rest of your life," Jerry added with his arms folded.

Wolman leaned forward and lowered his voice, "I'll need your help. I can learn a thing or two from an old football man like you."

Donohue regained his composure and sank into his office chair relieved and grateful for the best news his aging ears could've heard.

Jerry and Jiggs spent the rest of the afternoon recounting and separating the wheat from the chafe on the staff. Wolman was most pleased with Donahue's assessment and assistance.

As he opened Donahue's office door wide, Wolman shouted to create echoes. "The morale is miserable around here," Wolman declared looking around. "Let's say we give everybody a raise!" Donahue and the staff were floored in jubilation.

That night Jerry invited the entire organization out to a grand steak and lobster-fest dinner party at Bookbinder's. Two dozen of the Eagles' staff and Jerry's closest compatriots ate at the important VIP table in the bar area usually reserved for celebrities. Jerry and Anne sat with all the team's secretaries and executives as John Taxin proudly came by to toast Jerry. Wolman stood, raised his glass of Crown Royal and toasted his dear Philly friend right back. Taxin then took Jerry around the restaurant and introduced him to all of the other prominent guests. Back at the host's table, members of the former administration became acquainted and infused with the organization's new blood. Earl Foreman and his brother-in-law, Ed Snider also broke bread in high spirits. Earlier that day Ed had been named Treasurer of the team, fulfilling Jerry's previous promises.

Later, Jerry disappeared and made a cursory phone call as

cases of champagne were uncorked at the long table. Wolman then approached Taxin privately. On this huge night, Jerry proudly reached into his plentifully endowed pocket and handed the restaurateur a surprising set of shiny keys; Jerry's trademark show of appreciation. Only this time, when Jerry escorted John Taxin outside onto Walnut Street, Taxin was greeted by a genuinely jaw-dropping, tarp-covered harbinger of delight. With John's body frozen in front of the cloaked object, Jerry stepped to the restaurant owner's back and kneaded his neck.

"Thanks for all your help," expressed Wolman from the bottom of his heart. The cover was slowly drawn to expose a gift from Jerry to John: a brand new regal Rolls Royce Limousine.

*****

*Nearly eight months to the day later, Wolman went to work to discover that "Jiggs" Donahue had suffered a debilitating stroke, from which he never fully recovered. Being a part of the Eagles organization was Donahue's life, however, he was no longer able to perform his duties. Therefore, Jerry had a limousine pick up the disabled Jiggs from his home to take him to work each day. Personnel in the office enjoyed having Jiggs present, but the satisfaction and pleasure was all Donahue's. By early afternoon, Jerry would then have his driver take Jiggs home. As he had pledged from his very first day, Wolman caringly carried Donahue's salary for as long as he owned the team.*

# THE COACH

**P**rior to the Wolman era, Philadelphia had captured the NFL championship in 1960 when Norm Van Brocklin was the team's commander *and* chief at quarterback. Buck Shaw, the Eagles' victorious coach then decided to retire his clipboard while on top. All Philadelphia fans yearned for Van Brocklin to become the Bird's new coach. However, unable to hide his disdain for team management, the disgruntled quarterback was not favored with the job. Instead, Nick Skorich was brought in while fans cried in their cheesesteaks. The team enjoyed a 10-4 record in 1961 with Skorich, but then pitifully won only five of their next twenty-eight games under his leadership over the next two seasons. Wolman had purchased an NFL team mired in complete disarray and in shambles.

Following the dismal "2-12" 1963 campaign, one person who didn't receive a raise was Eagles head coach Nick Skorich. After meeting with "Jiggs" Donahue behind closed doors, Jerry knew what had become apparent to Skorich himself: the organization needed a new tactical philosophy and a more dependable strategy toward a winning direction. And so, Wolman's search for notable and skillful coaches began as the city's residents and media waited with bated breath.

Jerry flew to San Diego and met with Paul Brown, the former head coach in Cleveland. During the interview, Brown chewed upon some bitter seeds of a personal grudge with owner Art Modell who had just recently fired him. With focus on little else besides reaping vengeance on Modell, Brown used his interview with

Jerry to outline and detail the manner in which he could defeat his former Cleveland squad. Recognizing that there were thirteen other teams to upend, Wolman then assembled and spoke with reputable coaching candidates Otto Graham, Allie Sherman and George Allen. Allen, then the young talented defensive coach for the Chicago Bears, immediately connected with Jerry. George was a fierce and fiery competitor who gibed with Wolman's levels of intensity and passion for the game. Jerry was convinced he needed to look no further. A few days prior to formally announcing Allen as the team's head coach, Jerry received an unanticipated phone call from George Halas.

"I know that you're new to the league, so I'm going to give you some helpful advice," admonished Halas.

Jerry straightened behind his desk and listened intently.

"No one is more familiar with Coach Allen than I am here with the Bears. He's a solid *defensive* coach, don't get me wrong, but I just don't believe he'll ever make a good *head* coach in the league."

Wolman gulped awkwardly and silently, but thanked Halas for his honesty, claiming relief that he hadn't yet announced Allen as his choice at the helm.

*****

Joe Kuharich had been working at the NFL league office as supervisor of officials at the time the Eagles and Wolman came looking. He had served as head coach of the Chicago Cardinals in 1952 before becoming an NFL scout for several teams. In 1954-1958 he had coached the Washington Redskins for five seasons, and had been named "Coach of the Year" in 1955. He then returned to preside as the coach of his alma mater, Notre Dame from 1959 to 1962.

Wolman met with Kuharich several times, delving more deeply into his personality and his knowledge of the game. Jerry discovered that the solidly built, blunt man had been born in South Bend, Indiana, the son of an immigrant coal miner from Yugoslavia. He had avidly watched Knute Rockne and had played his collegiate ball for the Fighting Irish in the late 1930's. Kuharich then played two pro seasons in Chicago, but ceased pro ball to enlist in the Navy during World War II. The more Kuharich spoke, the more Wolman became enamored. Jerry empathized with each gridiron tale Kuharich told him, and could only surmise that this self-made "Joe" was a God-fearing, good family man, who really knew football. No other candidate had articulated his priorities in the order of faith, family and football as eloquently as had Kuharich. Jerry proudly hired Joe to a five-year, $35,000 per year contract.

Kuharich took over complete control of the football operations for the upcoming season and was also granted free reign in hiring his assistants. Weeks later, Dick Stanfel (offensive line), Fred Bruney (defensive backfield), Dick Evans (defensive line) and Herman Ball (offense) all joined the Eagle's nest determined to tirelessly prepare to transform the beaten-down organization into a winner.

*****

*Ten months later in Miami at the next NFL league meeting, Jerry ate lunch with George Halas and reminded him of their phone conversation about Coach George Allen. The Bears owner first chuckled, and then broke out laughing in the befuddled face of the munching rookie owner.*

*"I lied!" Halas ranted and convulsed at his own joke. "I just didn't want you to take our best young coach away from us!"*

# A Hero's Welcome

Almost a week after having successfully completed his grueling head coach search and signing, Jerry received a letter from the Mayor of Shenandoah, Albert J. Matunis.

"We'd like to give you an honorary diploma," it read. "Please join us for a *Welcome Home Jerry* extravaganza."

"An honorary diploma?" Jerry thought, gazing at the mayor's letterhead. Not having completed high school had always made Wolman feel incomplete. When Jerry shared the letter with his brother Manny, another proud hometown product, he was ecstatic over the news. The brothers lost no time regaling nostalgically over their childhoods. Jerry hung up the phone and responded to the mayor that an impromptu graduation and celebration would be an honor.

"However," Jerry asked Mayor Matunis, "would you make the extravaganza: Welcome Home Jerry *and Manny?*"

*****

A parade in Shenandoah was never a parody. For somebody important, it's the real McCoy. Henry Cabot Lodge had come through town when he was campaigning for Vice-President on the Nixon ticket in 1960. And so did presidential candidate John F. Kennedy, who passed through the coal region to the delight of large attentive crowds. But nothing could compare to an invitation to celebrate one of their own as the new owner of the Philadelphia Eagles, the fanatic football town's favorite team.

Days later, folks opened the *Shenandoah Evening Herald* to view no less than fifty ads highlighting the ceremonies while offering merchants' congratulations. Bold, thick headlines officially declared April 10th and 11th of 1964 as the two-day iconic gala event. The town worked into the night hanging banners, preparing parade routes and co-coordinating the closing of schools.

Jerry had retained two buses to carry his family members, staff and friends from Washington to Shenandoah that historic morning. When they arrived, nobody could have imagined what awaited them. Thousands upon thousands of people lined the streets, gallivanting at every turn. Wolman's group stepped out of the buses to glorious cheers and was led to a long motorcade of giant vehicular machines. Jerry, Anne, their children and Manny stood on the seats of a long open limousine convertible, followed by a line of massive polished fire engines. High upon the bright red fire trucks stood Jerry's bussed-in friends waving to the crowd. On another, Ed Snider wore a fireman's hat alongside the Eagles' Jim Gallagher, Joe King and Earl Foreman who took in the cheers as they held on for the rides of their lives. Jerry had arranged for yet another fire truck built as a float for those in his construction company. Men like Frank Bolek and Ed Dreyfuss nodded humbly with wide open smiles.

This was a hero's welcome like no other in Shendo. Jerry Wolman's ownership of the Eagles was to these crazed lifetime Birds' rooters bigger than if he'd found a bevy of diamonds in the anthracite mines. And they let him know it.

Seven Fire Departments' screeching sirens and swirling red and blue halogen headlights slowly drove through the town in a frenzy. On the streets, sequined majorettes pranced and glistened in short-skirted uniforms, screaming to lead the way. Alongside them young women twirled batons as high as overhead lampposts, while others shook golden long-haired pom-poms. The cheerleaders somersaulted and shimmied with their white-gloved hands on their stocking-hissing hips as if in a synchronized swimming competition. A two hundred-piece high school marching band preceded a regiment of every flag-carrying American Veteran from miles around. They strutted and saluted in full uniform to the deafening sounds of blaring brass horns and the crisp rasping rattle of snare drums.

Jerry looked around him at all that the town had prepared for him. He glanced at the joy on his brother's face and gleamed emotionally at the sight of his family, friends and business associates engrossed and gesturing over the cacophony of giant fire truck's growling engines.

"Hey Jerry, remember me?" many of those in the crowd called out. Every twenty seconds, Wolman ran from the convertible in order to shake hands with elderly women and men who'd known him as a rascal growing up, to whom he'd brought baskets on holidays, for whom he'd carried heavy bags of produce and groceries up stoops, and with whose sons and daughters he'd played. Jerry recalled each name, hugging the person and his own remembrance in one embrace.

All the Wolmans were flabbergasted at the unprecedented overflowing turnout, and they were even more overwhelmed when the parade swerved its path into the school yard of Jerry's almost-alma mater, J.W. Cooper High School. The entire student body and town's inhabitants had assembled in its auditorium where Superintendent John Downey announced that he was officiating at a ceremony to present Jerry his Honorary Graduation Diploma. Wolman was handed a cap and gown to a thunderous round of applause. Having waited twenty years, the sight of the gear brought tears to his eyes, wetting his cheeks, collecting in his dimples. Looking through the crowd, he saw Ms. Sampsell, his old grade school teacher seated near the front. Jerry blew her a kiss.

The high school "graduate" gave a splendid speech emphasizing the constant and kindest care he had received from Ms. Sampsell, blaming her gently for a good portion of his success. He acknowledged to the star-struck students the importance of staying in school and going to college.

Afterwards, Jerry's eleven-year-old son Alan took the stage to speak and show his pride about his wonderful father, now a belated-but-elated high school graduate. A photographer scampered to the front of the stage and snapped a picture of Jerry proudly holding his diploma in one hand and his son with the other. For Jerry, the whole day was like living through a fantasy of good fortune.

The parade and graduation ceremonies were only the beginning. The next day, the American Veterans' Hall had been newly bedecked with wall-to-ceiling posters of Jerry and his brother Manny. There, the brothers were feted with "keys to the city" and "lifetime memberships" in the Chamber of Commerce by the mayor and other prominent leaders.

By the midnight hour, Jerry was in his groggy glory. Holding Anne in his arms when rest finally came, he softly sang his old high school fight song to the tune of "On Wisconsin," into her fluttering eyes and tickling her ears romantically:

*"Shenandoah, Shenandoah, rush right through that line.*
*Round the ends and off the tackles, touchdown sure this time…*
*Rah! Rah!"*

After having experienced two days of exhilarating adulation, Jerry and Anne fell asleep soundly overcome. Their hearts swelled from the love of their friends and the sweet community they called home.

# CHANGES

Jerry flew into the Eagles' aerie the youngest owner in the NFL with high-flying visions. From the beginning he was determined, funded and equipped to launch a full-scale, first-class operation. Wolman had made up his mind: He would spare no expense in going above and beyond to take care of the Birds' organization, his employees and the fans.

Immediately, Wolman began looking for more desirable office space. By the summer of 1964, he found suitable digs at the old Bulletin Building located at 30th and Market Streets. It was an ideal spot because it was close to the press, nearer to Franklin Field and more than six times the former office's size in square footage. Jerry called upon Frank Bolek to promptly start interior renovations to house the have-it-all owner and his raring-to-go staff.

Commissioner Rozelle, Governor George David Lawrence, Art Rooney and four hundred standing-room-only guests and media invitees came across town to appear at the ribbon cutting thirty days later. The spectacularly spacious offices had been furnished with mahogany desks and surrounds, all of which were enveloped in walls painted Eagle green. White chair rails rallied in right angles at every turn.

Offices were constructed on both sides of two giant conference rooms. Long oval tables, shaped to resemble footballs, filled each conference area. Wolman had made certain to incorporate everyone in this luxuriously designed, unconfined place: coaches, ticketing sales persons, public relations personnel, secretaries and executives.

The exuberance attained was that of an immense happy family portrait where everyone was arranged to be seen and included.

As soon as the "Grand Opening" ceremonies had ended, and after the final slice of cake had been devoured, Jerry initiated a light football catch in the larger of the two conference rooms. What had begun as a friendly toss with his son Alan, soon erupted into wild horse-play. Jerry moved the football table in the room off to the side, and vigorously zipped the laced leather pigskin from one end of the room to the other. Stragglers curiously ventured to peek in and participate. Earl Foreman's glasses were nearly broken as a kicked football knuckled and veered by his nose as mischievous noises and laughter emanated from the carpeted field throughout the new offices.

Coach Kuharich looked in to see what all the fuss was about and shook his head at the youthful games and banter. Thick-skinned and unfazed, Kuharich had important work to do. The relocation of the Eagles' offices was not the only item on the makeover list receiving significant attention. Joe Kuharich and his assistant coaches were in the midst of making enormous off-season trades and acquisitions for new feathers to coat the Eagles.

Kuharich thereafter traded beloved star quarterback Sonny Jurgensen and safety Jim Carr to Washington, and spunky veteran wide receiver Tommy McDonald to Dallas. To improve a team with only two wins in the previous season, Kuharich acquired quality players such as Jim Ringo from Vince Lombardi's Packers' glory, former all-pro halfback Ollie Matson, defensive tackle Floyd Peters and quarterback Norm Snead. Some of the trades were as controversial to the press and fan base as the 1964 Gulf of Tonkin Resolution. Losing their perfectly armed, pot-bellied quarterback Jurgensen, was harder to swallow than a salty soft pretzel whole. But Wolman backed his new head coach one hundred percent. In fact, Dave Brady, a staff writer at the *Washington Post* reported of the Jurgensen for Snead trade that Kuharick had told the new owner, "Don't listen to those fans in the stands or you'll be up there with them."

Wolman never hesitated to ensure that those closely associated with his team would enjoy worriless contentment so that full attention could be on football. After having completed the new Eagles offices, he felt obliged to take care of all the people who filled them. Jerry moved out-of-towners to Philadelphia at his own expense, dramatically facilitating their relocation. In most cases, Jerry freely provided hefty down payments on many of his coach's new residences. With others, Wolman bought them their new houses outright. Wolman took special personal joy in helping his dear friends Johnny and Willie Robel purchase their home. Cascading his capital, Wolman richly rewarded high ranking Eagles' with astonishing perks.

At his core, Jerry Wolman simply loved getting to know people. The more time he spent with individuals, the more he loved them, and in particular, wished to see them prosper. His own "good times" had been the result of burdensome worry and staggering hard work with both shoulders to the grindstone. With a seemingly bottomless supply of money now in his coffers, he was able to afford what he wished: that his companions at the Eagles start without financial strains and remain on top.

One so bountifully blessed was Ed Snider. A long way from the D.C. street corner where Jerry had picked Ed and his spirits up, Snider now enjoyed an astoundingly high salary, entertainment expenses and personal use of the company limo and chauffeur. However, nothing meant more to the young team Treasurer than when Wolman had gifted Snider $83,000 for his down payment on a grand new home after also having made arrangements for his mortgage. In a sincerely grateful letter to his benefactor on September 4th, 1964, Snider wrote as follows:

> *"For the first time in my life, I have the desire to write a letter, the nature of which I have never had occasion to write before.*
>
> *Jerry, I got the biggest thrill in my life today - the combination of sitting in the little company and writing a check in excess of $83,000.00 for our new home while everyone's eyes popped out and of then going over to the home and realizing that this magnificent place would be where Myrna, the kids,*

*and I would be living.*

*All of this added to the exciting, challenging, and wonderful opportunity that you have given to me with the Eagles.*

*I only hope that my close association with you will give me the insight to acquire the many wonderful characteristics that you so naturally come by - generosity, consideration, humor, instinct, vast intelligence, unequalled common sense, humility, understanding - I could go on forever. Even more important is the fact that my overwhelming ambition is to see that you get much more than your money's worth.*

*Jerry, the finest thing that could happen to any man is to have you as a close friend – and the fact that this is the case with me overwhelms me dearly.*

*Having answered so many letters thanking you for this or that in the past year, I feel strange in writing one myself – but the simple spoken word could never adequately express my feelings – I just choke up.*

*There is nothing that is within my ability to do that I would not do for you, should you ask.*

*Eddie"*

\*\*\*\*\*

As the team began to form in the months leading up to the season, Jerry envisioned groundbreaking ideas to spruce things up and bring much more excitement for the fans. He hired bandleader Bill Mullin to swing his baton at an audition-selected 110-member professional marching band called "The Sounds of Brass." Then Wolman called for try-outs to assemble sixty physically talented women as "green and white" Eagle Majorettes and Cheerleaders.

One afternoon, Jerry and his fourteen-year-old daughter Helene attended the marching band's rehearsal.

Helene complained, "Why don't we have a war chant like the Redskins?"

"Why don't you write some words to a song and I'll give it to the band leader?" Jerry responded.

Having endured summer camp color wars, little Helene knew the cadences and style of a feisty fight song. A few weeks later, Helene Wolman handed her father this verse:

*"Fly Eagles fly, on the road to victory.*
*Fight, Green and White, score a touchdown 1, 2, 3...*
*Hit 'em low, Hit 'em high,*
*Watch our Eagles fly.*
*Fly Eagles fly, on the road to victory!*
*E- A- G- L- E- S, EAGLES!!!"*

*\*The song is still sung today at Eagles games after each Bird's touchdown.*

\*\*\*\*\*

Jerry was the last person to leave the new offices one evening, turning out their myriad lights. Before flipping the switch to his own office, he hesitated for a moment to look at the framed photograph he had snapped of Pablo Picasso during a recent trip to Italy. Picasso was wearing an Eagle's helmet and jersey that Jerry had exchanged with him for an original Picasso painting that hung next to the photo on the wall.

"Pretty damn unbelievable," he pinched himself and chuckled. Wolman thought how much he thrived on bringing about changes to the organization's personality. Jerry stepped to the doorway under the red illuminated "EXIT" sign mulling over the new accomplishments: the marching band, the Majorettes, the Cheerleaders, the big trades, the salaries, the raises and the lives he had touched.

In one fell swoop, before even a single football had been snapped, the Philadelphia Eagles were being transformed into an entity that mirrored the essence of its bedazzled, graciously grandiose owner. His fingers pushed down on the switch as the last light was extinguished.

"This is forever," Jerry wishfully muttered in the dark.

# Tackling Mayor Tate

O ne person notably absent from the new offices' ribbon cutting ceremonies was Philadelphia Mayor James H. J. Tate. From the day Jerry had arrived in town, the two locked horns over the portended placement of a new stadium to contain both major league baseball and football; i.e., the Phillies and the Eagles.

Before placing his winning bid on the team, Wolman had carefully reviewed well over fifty legal documents detailing the team's rights and obligations. One such document was the 1962 exclusive lease agreement signed by the mayor for the Eagles' football tenancy within a proposed new stadium. When Wolman and Tate had first conferred in October of 1963, the mayor affirmed all the terms of that agreement so that Wolman could depend upon it post-purchase.

Then in early 1964, as stadium talks began to escalate, everything literally changed. As the new Eagles owner, Jerry was called to meet with the mayor's proposed landlord, Ned Irish of Madison Square Garden Corporation, and other representatives from the mayor's staff. As quickly as Jerry extended his hand in pleasantries, he was abruptly greeted with a new lease agreement pressed into his open palm. Wasting little time, the entourage restlessly demanded he sign it. Wolman had been blindsided. Their proposal called for the building of a new stadium at 30th and Market Streets on stilts over the railroad, and more importantly reinvented the previously signed lease's clear language. The provisions Jerry had banked on called for an "8% of receipts" rental and exclusive football stadium rights for his team. The newly concocted lease proposed a graduated scale beginning at 10% of receipts and ballooned over time to heights upwards of 20%. Attached to the lease was a right-of-first-refusal clause in favor of the Madison Square Garden Corporation. Hidden in the fine print, the new rogue lease was to be non-exclusive for the Eagles football team.

Wolman seethed as his jaw locked. Unable to get comfortable in his seat, Jerry's first attempt at speaking was silenced by Ned Irish who tersely clamored, "It's non-negotiable." Wolman gazed around the room at the serious faces and frozen expressions of his adversaries. The group then threatened Wolman that if he did not comply, he could lose the right to play at Franklin Field, the team's current stadium. Again, there was silence. Jerry became incensed, stood up and refused to be "railroaded" by the engineers of the revised and mandated terms. Wolman stormed out.

Over the following weeks, Jerry received several threatening anonymous phone calls.

"I'm calling to do you a favor," the gruff voice said. "The mayor has told me that unless you play at 30th and Market Stadium, he will take Franklin Field away from you."

Disturbed by the multiple cautionary "warnings," Jerry called for a private meeting with Mayor Tate. At their conference in "Hizzoner's" office, Tate coldly reiterated every Irish revision and was adamant about each. Wolman smelled a rat. Rumors had swarmed that the mayor had favored some of those men who'd lost the bid for the Eagles, for reasons known best to politicians. By proposing an exclusive stadium lease to the Phillies but a non-exclusive lease to the Eagles, it was apparent to Wolman that the mayor may have had ulterior plans and motives. Allegations whirled that Tate now favored a group of his friends in bringing an AFL team to Philadelphia.

Face to face, the two men squared off. Jerry began:

"Mayor, it seems under those terms and conditions, it's impossible for us to ever entertain going into a stadium that was not voted on by the majority of taxpaying people."

"Look Wolman," the mayor chastised, "why don't you worry about the Eagles and I'll worry about the taxpayers."

Wolman quickly snapped back, "Mayor, I'll be glad to let you worry about the taxpayers as long as you remember I'm one of them!"

Jerry was cognizant of the strong opposition to the "30th Street stadium" by some members of City Council, a few powerful civic groups including the University of Pennsylvania and Drexel University. Wolman likewise felt that the site was completely wrong. He preferred wide open areas in South Philadelphia to house the sports teams, with easier access and better parking facilities. Most importantly, he would not even consider a lease without exclusive rights for his Eagles and bereft of any first-refusal legal albatrosses. After all, twenty-one of the twenty-two pro football clubs had enjoyed exclusive leases at their stadiums.

It took Jerry no time to understand the mayor's underlying threat to the Eagles. He also realized that the soon-to-expire Phillies' lease was being used as a bargaining chip against Bob Carpenter, the baseball team's owner, who had nowhere else to play. Tate's forces were placing the Phillies in a vise and tightening it.

In order to gain leverage and protect the Phillies' lease, Wolman arranged on June 23rd, 1964 to purchase Connie Mack Stadium from J.A. Schliefer Properties of New York for $757,500 after just ten minutes of negotiations. Jerry called a relieved Carpenter to advise him that the Phillies had a home for as long as the baseball club wanted, certainly until a new stadium was ready. Wolman had already quietly asked Carpenter to join him in developing a stadium in South Philadelphia with their own raised funds, leaving City Hall in the dust. Wolman's bald, brassy buy of Connie Mack Stadium rendered the mayor powerless in his leverage over the Phillies. Tate now realized he had no financial sway whatsoever over Wolman.

Jerry's focus was on football and he was in no mood to play politics: neither to gain political favors for himself nor allow others to be given them. He'd never in the past allowed politicians to rule his whereabouts or wherewithal. To Jerry, the people of his newly adopted city deserved more, and he could afford to stand solidly in line with his principles. Wolman was determined to fight.

The battle intensified and was heightened when Tate attempted to discredit Wolman publicly. Claiming that Jerry had purchased

Connie Mack Stadium in order to demolish it and build the new stadium over it in North Philadelphia, the mayor charged that Wolman was simply attempting to reap huge personal financial gains. He called Jerry to task for wanting an exclusive agreement for the Eagles, claiming no such deal had ever been decided upon in the past. Tate described the little-known Wolman as a rude rube who blocked deals for his own lucrative rewards and stormed out of meetings with little or no regard for the fans in Philadelphia.

Following the mayor's barrage of denigration, Jerry had heard, read and seen enough. Seeking vindication, the volatile owner was determined to set the record straight. He called for a press conference.

On an early summer's eve, Jerry carefully positioned himself behind tens of microphones placed near his face by the city's press, television and radio stations, on a podium festooned by an Eagle's head in the center of a spotlighted stage.

He cleared his throat and proclaimed, "I insist that the promise made to the Eagles of exclusivity must be kept."

Wolman held up the mayor's signature on the previously signed exclusive lease as if it were a rally-towel, silencing the crowd by the audacity of the maneuver. Jerry bluntly and succinctly set forth the truth, and emphasized in no uncertain terms that the mayor was indeed a "liar."

Jerry had cleared the air from under Billy Penn's hat, in effect tipping it by introducing himself to the citizenry of the city. He was not one to turn the other cheek when facing a falsehood.

Wolman paused to allow the gasps to continue, then completely dispelled another untruth by doing the garishly unthinkable. To counter the mayor's claims that he'd been acting out of self-profit and greed, Jerry publicly offered to sell Connie Mack Stadium to the city for fifty cents, so long as the Phillies' occupancy was protected. The mayor scoffed at the offer calling it "childish." But Wolman was serious.

"Be careful, mayor," Jerry warned with a grin, "this *child* follows through on what sometimes seems like pretty wild ideas."

In the end, transparency and the truth prevailed. Jerry had played hardball with Tate in order to prove to Philadelphians that their best interests were not to be tampered with by favoritism in the political arena. The bar for actions by professional sports teams in Philadelphia had been raised. After months of Tate's hassling to save face and each side's threats of law suits, Mayor Tate gave in. The Broad and Pattison Streets' South Philly site was selected in order to benefit the respective exclusive rights of each club without interference or conniving with the political moguls of mediocrity.

Jerry's biggest battle and his toughest opponents, cronyism and misuse of political power, had been soundly tackled even before the kick-off of his first game of professional football.

# HERSHEY - 1964

The summer months of 1964 brought unbearable waves of heat to Philadelphia. The Eagles opened pre-season training camp in mid-July at nearby Hershey, Pennsylvania to temperatures that made the town's famous chocolate bars melt and bubble in the hands of its children.

Two hundred and sixty-five pound linemen in pads and helmets, harnessed into green jerseys, walked onto the recently mowed grass of the football playing field knowing they would shed fifteen pounds before the first Eagles practice had ended. The fresh smell of the grass placated none of the players as they stretched to get loose and sweat began to pour.

Scooting onto the field at the fifty yard line was a high-kicking sprinter in sweat-pants with a smile much too jolly for so solemn an occasion.

"Yo, hey buddy!" the largest of the cautiously strolling linemen called out from the ten yard stripe to the runaway renegade. "We're gonna practice here in a minute. Get off the field!"

Johnny Robel, the team's equipment manager, picked up a football and flung it to the out-of-place route-runner racing down the sidelines toward the players.

With a gesture of non-linguistic clarity, the confused lineman snapped the towel from around his neck at the rogue runner as the latter dashed by making a rousing over-the-shoulder catch. The receiver let out a cackle and gripped the leather ball proudly. He turned the laces upward and gazed at its professional label.

"Who is that guy?" asked the giant lineman with hot curiosity. One of his mates moaned lowly, "That's the new owner."

*****

Jerry felt like a babe in the woods and a kid in a candy store at training camp. He had been spearheading his entrance onto the sports scene with frequent speaking engagements, all the while fidgety with anticipation for play to begin. He'd also spent hours upon hours pre-quelling "hard-hat" construction project issues to allow himself the luxury of wearing his football fairy tale "owner's crown." All he could think of through May and June was getting to Hershey for the players' arrival.

On the sweltering morning of that afternoon's advent of team personnel, Jerry decided to drive his motorcycle rather than his brand new Mercedes from Philadelphia to Hershey. He wanted to be able to get around the town without fuss and he didn't want the players to think he was showy. Wolman genuinely wanted to fit in with his team.

After checking into his room, he wandered around on foot feeling like a lost soul at the gates of his own heaven, except for the fact it was so abnormally hot.

When he arrived in camp offices, the coaches didn't seem to need him while they busily worked out practice schedules and routines. No one consulted him or seemed to have any cause to. Wolman felt as if he were a kingfish out of water. But when the pro's arrived that day, things changed in a hurry. Jerry was once again on the job-site working with his men.

The green owner got the feel of the intensity of two-a-day practices, grunting along with team in unison. He never missed a minute of push-ups, sprints, cumbersome calisthenics or contact drills. He attended teaching sessions at defensive and offensive linemen meetings with the coaches. What he had thought he knew about football, he now knew didn't even scratch a screeching blackboard's chalked surface. It wasn't long before he started filling in for a defensive end or a wide-out receiver if the team was short someone for the down. The patron saint of professional football had opened up the surly pearly gates of heaven where everyone wore black shoes and cleats. The blessed owner stood well above the clouds of everyday life.

On some evenings, when all had departed the practice field, Jerry and Johnny Robel would re-enact their Shendo plays from long ago memories. Both counted down the seconds during an imaginary childhood game, winding perilously close to its final seconds. The sound of a real starter's pistol going off to finalize the matter could not have stopped their reverie.

The camp rigors were draining as the weather never let up. A plethora of salt pills were swallowed while quart jugs of iced water were dumped under jerseys and over heads. The weak faltered and were cut; the strong held on and survived to make the team's final rounds of competition. Fights erupted and no one stopped them.

"Let them go, it's good for them," the coaches callously figured. In the end, peace reigned, but the measure of a man had been taken and noted.

"Lights out" finished the players' evening's studious play-book lessons in exchange for a sound body-regrouping sleep. Jerry and the coaches headed for Ballantine and Miller drafts at local bars to discuss football, the only topic about which anyone cared. Burgers and fries were devoured past midnight as names of players were bandied about with connotations of capabilities. Conversations ended with what was needed for the next day. Jerry always relished the next day's events, knowing he'd be at the center of them.

Finally the day arrived for the Eagles' first pre-season home game against the Washington Redskins. On August 7th, 1964, the field thermometers were registering mercury above a hundred degrees. Wolman chose not to sit in the owner's box for his premiere professional game. Rather, he preferred watching alongside coaches Fred Bruney and Mike Nixon from their vantage point high in the coach's box. There, Bruney and Nixon could work the spotting phones and signal to Kuharich's staff at game level.

The Eagles were burned at the stake that day by the Redskins 37-0, a score borne out by maliciously inspired predictions of the press and fans after Kuharich had traded Sonny Jurgensen to the Washington club. The drudging left the usually cheerful owner in a dreadful state; embarrassed, disheartened and distraught.

Moreover, from the moment of kickoff until the game's final play, three hecklers in their late thirties or early forties had emigrated near the press box. Seated just below Jerry and his coaches, the men continuously called out loudly and profanely while razzing and deriding Kuharich and his team. All of Wolman's family and many of his friends had come to Hershey for the game and were accommodated close to the field in ear-shot of the rabble-rousers. Even after the interminable massacre on the field had ended, the hecklers continued their barrage in the stands with abandon.

Wolman, unused to losing and almost tearful, made his way along the bleachers' steps toward Anne Wolman and their daughter Helene. After a few downtrodden strides, he heard one of the big-mouthed brigands yell, "A JEW should not own a football team! The game's too rough for their little white hands!"

The men continued their vile liturgy, then abruptly turned and faced Wolman's wife and daughter.

"Jews shouldn't own the Philadelphia Eagles!" the men yelled in chorus at Anne as Jerry approached.

Upon seeing his defenseless wife and daughter subjected to the hateful rants, Wolman erupted like a lava loaded volcano. He darted at the men and began swinging with a Shenandoah shower of fists. Within seconds, Wolman had struck the jaws of all three "big-mouths" as teeth took off into the humid air in all directions. When the men fought back, Jerry grabbed their shirts and pulled them down the bleachers tumbling with him, as the crowd in the stands scrambled and screamed. Jerry managed some well-placed kicks at groins and elbows at brains as the battling crew smacked against each row of stands with the snowballing forces of speed and gravity.

"Jerry!" Anne screamed repeatedly as others came to the owner's aid.

Coach Bruney joined the fray throwing a flurried array of rapid punches from his heels, and Manny Wolman landed a few jabs and caught a few others. Almost immediately, players Bob Brown, Maxie Baughn and Israel Lang, Kuharich's son Larry, Johnny Robel and the police disentangled the Rubik's Cube of fighters as they reached the ground in a melee.

Wolman wound up in the locker room with three broken ribs. Anne Wolman was near collapse from fright and worry, but ministered to her husband while shaking and trembling in disbelief.

Al Nelson, a rookie defensive back, had never encountered a scene like this.

"Is that my owner? This is a madhouse," the rookie back described the three-minute spectacle.

The veteran players had new respect for Jerry. They kidded him for years afterward that they would never even think of getting into a fight against him, nor ever entering a fight without him. Dispelling any stigma surrounding his wealth and his age, Jerry had found a way to fit in with his team.

Wolman was fined an unprecedented $10,000 by the league, a sum larger than most players' annual salaries. It stung even more when Walter Annenberg, the powerful owner of one of Philadelphia's daily newspapers, the *Inquirer*, and the city's phenomenal philanthropist, called Jerry onto the printing press carpet. Annenberg lectured him face to face, "that a nice Jewish boy shouldn't act like that." Jerry apologized with his head bowed.

During the remainder of training camp, a new lucrative T.V. contract was announced that created a surprisingly large monetary bonus for NFL teams. Whereas Jerry first believed he'd be losing approximately $250,000 per year, he would presently make a $700,000 profit through his first year.

The $10,000 reprimand seemed like a mere wrap on the wrist. His ribs hurt less too.

# THE 1964 SEASON

**P**rior to opening the regular season, Wolman was a basket case of anxiety and nerves. Etched on the Eagles schedule for the first game of the 1964 season was a "David versus Goliath" match-up against the reigning NFL champion New York Giants.

On September 13th, 1964, sixty thousand football loyalists flocked to see their new-look Eagles fly. Jerry arrived at the stadium with his wife and daughter in a mind-numbing stupor. Wolman perused the field and saw his son Alan throwing a football to Johnny Robel. He waived at his twelve year-old child with pride. The extended hand of Commissioner Rozelle awakened him from the sight of his son's smile.

"Welcome to the league," began Rozelle. Wolman was honored that the Commissioner chose to attend his first game when thirteen other teams were likewise kicking off their season that same day. The youthful owner shook the dynamic Commissioner's hand with tremendous respect.

Excitement had reached meteoric levels as the brand new 110-person "Sounds of Brass" marching band high-kicked in long strides onto Franklin Field. The spectacle and sounds of uniforms and instruments were as loud as each other, pounding forth the musical proposition that a bright silver lining had circled the Eagles playing field with nary a cloud in sight.

The opposing team was introduced first over a loudspeaker system made faint by the band's tubas. Y.A. Tittle, the Giants quarterback, shuttled his rugged frame onto Franklin Field to sonorous boos as fans placed more relish in their vocal abhorrence of opponents than they did on their hot dogs.

Pacing restlessly before the game, Wolman had been soothed to a teetering calm by Coach Kuharich.

"Relax, Jerry," the coach said out of the side of his mouth. "We've got some surprises in store they've never seen before."

The Eagles, however, remained double-digit underdogs in the betting pools. The team's pre-season losses and both teams' prior years' performances enhanced the odds against the Birds. No one gave them a chance.

With a sudden explosive boom, the new era began as the hometown heroes jetted out of the tunnel and onto the field through a mist of green smoke pumped into the Sunday air. The rowdy crowd set off a palpable rush that rustled through the stands.

Wolman's stomach muscles tightened with tension as he sat adjacent to the Commissioner in the press box. The nearby reporters and photographers nodded to Jerry sympathetically. They were already preparing their story to write off his team against the defending NFL champs. As the Giants kicked off to the home team, all nervousness left Wolman's psyche. He knew the heart of his men and had stupendous faith in his head coach.

The Eagles returned the opening kick to their own 41 yard line. In a blink, on the first play from scrimmage, fullback Earl Gros ran 59 yards for a touchdown. Wolman watched in jubilant disbelief as the Eagles were soaring with claws extended. The remainder of the game was an astonishing landslide. Kuharich's defense had rattled Tittle with hidden blitzes from all angles as the coach's elaborate schemes evolved into a violent geometry lesson. Tittle was sacked seven times with crunching forearms and swooping full-bodied tackles. The Giants quarterback was removed from the game in the fourth quarter out of bloody necessity to the delight of the rollicking fanatics in the stands. At the sound of the final gun, the transformed Eagles had rocked and slain the mighty Giants by a score of 38-7.

Hundreds surrounded Jerry in congratulations. Flashbulbs flickered so quickly it seemed as if all participants were in a silent movie. Unable to contain his glee, Wolman raced onto the field aimlessly and put his arms around his coach. Anne, Helene and Alan rushed to meet Jerry with hugs, kisses and laughing tears.

"That was easy," joked Jerry seriously, while hugging and kissing back.

In the locker room after the game, Captain Maxie Baughn stood up in his pads, "Today we want to present the game ball to somebody we think deserves it, someone we've all grown close to, and has grown close to us."

Baughn threw Wolman the ball as the players cheered and kept cheering all through their showers.

That night the Wolmans and the coaches had a celebration dinner at Bookbinder's restaurant among five pound lobsters and highrise slices of cherry cheesecake. When the undefeated owner entered the restaurant, he was greeted by thunderous applause and a standing ovation. Steady streams of people wanted autographs in between courses. There was no happier man on earth than Jerry Wolman.

*****

Jerry soon learned that not all NFL games would be glorious victories. The following week the team suffered a close loss to San Francisco. A win, no matter the manner it was achieved, left Wolman on a euphoric high for days feeling as if he had defeated the world. Conversely, a loss was debilitating to him.

Walking by the press conference after the loss, Jerry struggled as the questioners bit into his coach and his players with poisonous venom. From day one, the media had never coveted the selection of Kuharich.

"Unmerciful," agonized Jerry watching on from the side as threatening buzzard-shaped clouds of reporters circled above his coach's head.

Even when the Eagles weren't achieving wins, their owner was bringing about a new persona for the team. Jerry purchased over three hundred tickets and six enormous buses to transport fans from his hometown Shenandoah and the surrounding towns of the coal region to enjoy an Eagles game set for November 22nd, 1964. He called it "Anthracite Day," commemorating the days when he'd hitchhiked to games as a youngster with no ticket to take.

Chauffeured fans poured in from Frackville, Pottsville, Mahanoy City and Shenandoah that Sunday to take in a rare professional game. Several mayors from the coal region presented Wolman with a hefty anthracite clock during a ceremony at mid-field before the contest. Despite the owner's gesture, the then 5-5 Eagles were soundly defeated.

The Philadelphia Eagles finished 6-8 in third place that year after having finished seventh (last) the previous two seasons. In spite of the progress, "JOE MUST GO" signs appeared everywhere blatantly slighting the head coach. One home game was marred by a banner-pulling single engine plane carrying the three callous words on aerial display. The slogan became the mantra of the contemptuous crowd below.

Jerry admired his coach and regarded his relationship with Kuharich as family. Wolman's experiences and values mandated that the most essential ingredient in any enterprise was loyalty.

A particularly excruciating public bashing occurred after a heartbreaking 2-point loss in St. Louis, in the final game of the season. Jerry decided that he had to take the heat off of his coach. Afterwards Wolman announced he'd give Coach Kuharich an unprecedented 15-year contract and name him the team's General Manager, raising his salary by $15,000.

A tidal wave of shock crashed over the press. The team's owner had finally discovered a way to momentarily silence the critics. And they weren't the only ones caught up in astonishment.

Wolman was concerned that the raise showed preferential treatment for Kuharich over Snider, both of whom had been at odds over the direction of the team. To compensate, Jerry raised Snider's salary, granted a contract extension and elevated him as a Vice President. But a rivalry had begun and a noticeable crevice had been established. Jerry was too happy and too busy to worry. Money seemed to smelt together the creeping cracks in the silver lining.

The only other way to fix matters was to win. And the Eagles did more winning that season than in the previous two years combined. Wolman had led the franchise to an encouraging resurgence of respectability. Moreover, he did it with a certain flair for grandiosity.

# The Heart Of The Owner

Jerry used his glad and abundantly grateful disposition during the much improved season of 1964 by upgrading the whole team's mind-set. He became the first owner in football to charter his own plane with United Airlines for his players' flights to and from games, with steaks on the way to games, and steaks served with cold beers for the ride home. Unlike other franchises, Wolman's team stayed only in first class hotel accommodations, pampered with the finest food and amenities.

The owner also engulfed himself in a private Queen Air 12-seater plane for commuting with his family and friends back and forth from Washington and Philadelphia, learning to pilot the plane himself. He also purchased a breathtaking race-winning boat or two, whose liberal use was assigned to kind business associates for their pleasure.

One of the more stirring perks of his powerful whirlwind was the national fame that now followed in his footsteps. Soon everyone wanted to be acquainted with Jerry Wolman, including a cabal of celebrities. Dionne Warwick came around the team offices often as she was dating Eagle running back Timmy Brown. Milton Berle, a friend of John Taxin, became the Eagles mascot for a few games, energizing the crowd with sideline antics. Gregory Peck, a football devotee, became a close friend. And even a young Cassius Clay was brought to Jerry to manage the boxer's career. Although the undertaking appealed to Wolman, Commissioner Rozelle persuaded Jerry not to get involved in the boxing domain.

"Look at me! Look at me! I own the Eagles!" mocked Don Rickles clapping his hands, while over-exuberantly hopping haphazardly around the stage at the luminous Latin Casino in New Jersey.

Shecky Green, Jack Benny, George Burns, Jackie Gleason, Red Buttons, Jimmy Durante, Sammy Davis, Jr. and Frank Sinatra became Wolman favorites for socializing. One Saturday night in Las Vegas, Sinatra's eyes grew bluer as he grabbed Jerry by the arm and pulled him aside. Frank complimented Jerry on his "three-jaw" preseason punch and altercation in the bleachers of Hershey. "I like you, kid. You don't act like an owner. You're a tough son-of-a-bitch!"

Running the Eagles was like no other business in which Jerry had ever been involved. He knew it was an ego trip, but nothing diverted his attentiveness away from his responsibilities to the sporting life of the city and to the people of Philadelphia. Jerry went out of his way to express his gratitude for what sportsmen of Philadelphia teams had brought to the city, and how much he was reaping benefits from their hard work. Likewise, he was simply devoted to the hard-nosed and knowledgeable sports fans throughout Philadelphia and its environs.

There were thousands upon thousands of letters from fans writing compliments, and even some detractors noting his debacles. Wolman answered every one. Never was a request for an autograph declined. Letters poured in seeking donations, sponsorships, speaking assignments and requests to serve on Boards of Directors. The only letters to which Jerry remained mute were those which threatened him with bad luck and curses if he wouldn't send a stash of cash.

Many of the letters were heart-wrenching, by people who were truly in need of help. Jerry assigned Arnold Stark on his staff to determine fact from fiction, and then allowed his wealth to do good things, often anonymously and many times in cash. Wolman had heard a synagogue sermon whose lesson he had taken to heart. The rabbi's credo was laconic and direct, "To do good is *good*."

Jerry lived by the credence that success had to be shared. Therefore, he made it a point of personal concern to help others whom he liked or who were in need. And many of his deeds were often life-changing to others.

One afternoon during the season, Wolman approached Bill Mullin, the bandleader who was brooding in the Eagles' office lobby.

"Bill, what's wrong?" Jerry inquired. Mullin was a hardworking employee who had performed capably with the team's marching band unit. He was also one of the kindest souls at the Eagles. The two men slowly marched to Jerry's office and closed the door.

"I'm having serious financial problems," Mullin shared uncomfortably with the team owner. "The banks are foreclosing on my house."

Jerry interrupted Mullin with a most unexpected solution. "Bill, don't worry," Wolman placated, "I'll pay off your Note."

A few weeks later, Mullin invited his closest friends to a "Mortgage Burning" party at the home he was to keep. Business Manager Joe King, Coach Kuharich and others, as well as Anne and Jerry stood in the bandleader's backyard alongside Mullin's wife and children. Jerry was asked to do the honor of setting a lit match to the paid six-figure mortgage.

The recipients of Wolman's kindnesses were not always people known to him, just people he felt would appreciate what small effort he could make on their behalf.

On cold winter days, Wolman stopped on a dime upon seeing a young newspaper boy standing behind a stack of newspapers.

"How much you want for all of them?" he asked.

"Excuse me, Sir?" the boy's lips quivered.

"I'd like to purchase all of your newspapers."

The dumbfounded paperboy thought to himself and looked back at his stack, "Ten dollars."

Jerry handed the youth a sizzling twenty dollar bill. "Now go on home and get yourself warm."

Wolman never received greater satisfaction than seeing the stunned look of elation on a youngster's face. And he constantly spoke at charitable events for children as if it were a crusade.

*****

Neither was Wolman the type of man to turn his back on a damsel in distress. After the conclusion of an Eagles meeting in Philadelphia, he was to fly back to Washington, D.C. that afternoon amidst a treacherous storm. Walking through Philadelphia International Airport to get to his parked private plane, Jerry noticed a distraught young woman in her early twenties seated in the terminal crying. When he approached and asked her if she was okay, he learned that due to the bad weather, her flight had been cancelled. The poor lass was desperate to reach Richmond, Virginia. She was meeting a young man for the first time for a highly recommended and much anticipated blind date. Jerry listened to the young woman's romantic tale of two strangers exchanging letters and talking on the phone. But they had not yet met in person. No matter how hard Jerry tried, he could not restrain the young lady from crying. At the moment just before Wolman himself felt a tear coming on, he offered, "I'll fly you. Let me take you to Richmond."

The stranded traveler stopped weeping at once. It's possible the girl didn't actually believe the proposition until she saw the private plane and the pilot step out to greet Jerry.

Wolman and his guest rode to Washington, D.C. together in a storm that seemed gentler once everyone's plans were secured. Upon reaching the nation's capital, Jerry left for his home and gave the pilot directions and flight plans to Richmond. Of course, Wolman never saw the young woman again. However, he did receive a letter several years later from an attorney who thanked Jerry, claiming he was forever indebted to him for steering his wife and the love of his life to him in a storm.

$$*****$$

Among businessmen, Jerry was always on full alert to be helpful to ambitious men with great ideas. A week following Wolman's first game's shellacking of the New York Giants, Jerry was handed the footage shot on 16-millimeter film by Ed Sabol, the owner/producer of the fledgling Blair Motion Picture Company. The film, entitled "The Start of Something Big," artistically captured the Eagles' victory glorifying the game, its aesthetic physical beauty and grueling emotions. Sabol was one who had the inclination and expertise to film and produce play-by-play NFL games in the theatrical style of a Hollywood movie reel. Wolman appreciated the gesture and was sold by what he saw.

Pete Rozelle had wanted to sign Sabol prior to Jerry's purchase of the Eagles, but he failed to convince the owners. The problem had been that each owner would have had to invest $12,000 for the merger to occur. Very few wished to. When Jerry arrived on board, the Commissioner asked him to figure a way to have the other owners accept a Sabol-run filming operation in conjunction with the league.

The matter was put on the agenda after the close of the 1964 season during a league meeting at the Kenilworth Hotel in Miami, Florida. Wolman voted in favor of the Sabol-NFL combo, but others held out again due to a key point at issue: Owners were contra the Ed Sabol transaction because the film-maker was working without a realistic place to operate professionally as befits an NFL affiliate. Wolman listened in silence to the owners' wrangling over Sabol's lack of proper accommodations required for the magnitude of the endeavor. The Eagles owner stood his ground and declared he'd put the objection to bed.

"I'll buy a building in which Sabol can operate."

With that proactive and positive support, the next vote carried in Sabol's favor to give birth to what was to be named "NFL Films." Jerry spent nearly $250,000 to acquire the North 13th Street building in downtown Philadelphia. It was a grand building which included a former theater that was perfect for the enterprise. The iconic NFL venture was housed rent-free for its first year in business, and "anything" that could be paid thereafter.

"Whatever you can afford, and whenever you can afford it," said Jerry. Wolman sensed that this collaboration would indeed be the start of something big. Bolstered by the voice-over of legendary baritone-bar-none, John Facenda, the visual and audio game renditions of NFL Films were superior to any in sports annals. Ed Sabol and his son Steve have maintained the highest quality since. Without Wolman's foresight and promotional prescience, the competence of the Sabols, and Facenda's majestic voice of Moses reading the Ten Commandments, football could not have been as precious to its followers and disciples.

NFL Films remained in the site until 1981. The company is recognized as an American institution. In 2009, a Commonwealth of Pennsylvania historic marker was planted just outside the landmark building.

*****

*"Jerry Wolman has a special place in the history of NFL Films. His generosity and foresight gave us the chance to grow and succeed. He is the unsung hero in the story of our company."*

-Steve Sabol
President of NFL Films

# Chicago – 1964

While the Philadelphia Eagles passionately filled Jerry's being, he never compromised his first love: building. By the late spring of 1964, he was about to embark on his grandest structural undertaking.

In 1963, Ted Dailey, now Jerry's longtime loan correspondent, decided to accept a new job as a proprietor running Advance Mortgage Company in Chicago. Before he did so, however, he met with Wolman. Ted asked that if he ever got into a problem writing mortgages, would Jerry come to his rescue in the Windy City and make a few fee-generating deals. Dailey made it clear he would not accept the new position otherwise, and Jerry readily agreed.

Business initially went well for Ted, but a downturn in the real estate financing market jilted and jolted him in early 1964. There were a few scarce available properties scattered through the Midwest metropolis, so he called his dear friend Jerry, "I need your help."

Wolman flew out the next morning to Chicago, a city he'd never been in before. After meeting at the airport, the men drove to six properties for consideration. Unfortunately, none of them appealed to Jerry's sense of sound, solid investments, nor did anything ignite his mind's eye. He felt wilted letting down his friend. After having endured an arduous day of prospecting, the two headed back toward Ted's office. While driving down Michigan Avenue, Jerry's attention became immediately transfixed on what appeared to be a massive, fenced city block. A sign advertising the First National Bank of Chicago was raised above the fencing.

"Who owns *that* property?" Jerry asked, struck by this inadvertent discovery.

"John Mack," downplayed Dailey. "It's not for sale, or at least no one's been able to buy it."

The property was ideally located along Michigan Avenue's "Miracle Mile" next to the famed Chicago Water Tower. Wolman instantly felt energized by the possibilities and vision of a major structure at this site.

Jerry promptly telephoned John Mack as he sat behind Dailey's desk a moment after arrival. Mack recognized Wolman's name from having read about the Eagles acquisition, and took the call.

"Mr. Mack, I'd like to buy your property," Jerry began, wasting no words.

"You and everyone else," undercut Mack. "But everyone haggles and has lists of contingencies."

Jerry realized he had to act quickly. He asked the reluctant owner what he wanted for the land.

"$5,000,000," barked back Mack, "with a half-million dollar deposit and a completed contract to sign within forty-eight hours."

"Done," pounced Wolman, "I'll have your deposit tomorrow." Jerry requested an allowance for a short time to check upon the zoning for economic feasibility and for borings in the ground to ensure the soil's proficiency to support a major building.

The two men orally agreed and a deal was made. Jerry hung up the phone to let out a holler. Wolman's hot hands clasped Dailey's stunned, cold fingers. Next, Jerry called Earl Foreman. Wolman required his attorney to pick up a certified check from American National Bank for $500,000 and fly to Chicago the next day to commence preparations for a written Agreement of Sale. Within the Mack-mandated timeframe, the contract was signed.

Prior to affixing signatures, Jerry had contacted the firm of Skidmore, Owings and Merrill, a prestigious architectural/engineering firm to garner and glean the information he needed. Dailey and Wolman met with SOM's architects Nathanial Owings and Bruce Graham. By the end of his conference, Jerry had hired the firm. Graham was specifically assigned to lead the project.

"I need to know as soon as possible what can be built on the site under the present zoning," Wolman pressed.

Within a week, after having tended to his family, attended Eagles meetings and after having placed all building projects in respectable order, Jerry flew back to Chicago in June to meet with Graham. Wolman was shown numerous sketches of two narrowly adjacent buildings positioned on the Michigan Avenue land for anticipated construction. The architect informed Wolman that a 40-story office building aside a 70-story apartment building would be permissible under the present zoning. While Graham sat across from Wolman verbally relaying the potential square footage figures, Jerry listened and concurrently calculated the rental parameters. He realized that he had transacted a steal of a deal. His computer-like analysis of the flow of money convinced Jerry that the land was worth double what he had just agreed to pay for it. As the dollar signs rapidly multiplied in his mind, Wolman was most assured that he was embarking on a financially fortuitous, hugely bountiful enterprise.

During the first half of the 1960's decade, Wolman had been John Hancock Mutual Life Insurance Company's fair-haired golden boy. Jerry was Hancock's number one client and largest borrower. The Company had persistently and eagerly solicited his bustling business. Following the meeting with Graham, Jerry asked Ted Dailey to submit a package to John Hancock by which Jerry would (1) sell the Company his land for $6,000,000, provided it would lease it back to him for sixty years at a reasonable rent; (2) give Jerry options to buy back the land at a nominal price upon certain timed intervals; and (3) make a one hundred percent loan to Jerry to construct the edifices.

Dailey scoffed at the sugary-sweet deal. "John Hancock will never go for it," he shook his head side to side.

But Hancock did. Ten days later, an incredulous Dailey, shaking his head up and down, proclaimed that Hancock had agreed to Wolman's terms with a principal loan of the total cost equaling $63,000,000. Jerry was suddenly at the center of the biggest real estate deal in the country. At closing, Hancock paid Jerry $6,000,000 for the land from which he paid $5,000,000 to John Mack. Without having spent one penny out of pocket, Wolman had lined his own with $1,000,000.

In July, Dailey again called Wolman, but this time with a worrisome tone. Judge Byron K. Elliott, Chairman of the Board of Hancock, had requested to meet with Jerry. Wolman flew to Boston to see the reputedly intimidating judge.

"My Board Members are concerned that the site is too crowded," he stated with a noticeable lisp. "What can you do to loosen up the site?"

To a builder, "loosening up" meant only one thing: to build smaller. Smaller meant less square footage, and therefore less profit. Jerry asked for more time.

He flew back to Chicago with his friend and business partner, Sidney Teplin, to meet with Bruce Graham and Ted Dailey at an Italian restaurant for lunch. Upon hearing the judge's complaint, Graham became adamant against the notion of going smaller.

"We can't do anything!" he roared. "It would be uneconomical!"

"Bruce," calmed Jerry, "I don't want to lose the loan or this project with Hancock. Let's think of something."

The four men tore apart pieces of bread and dipped them in saucers of olive oil on the table. They sat pondering silently, discouraged for ten long seconds. Out of the corner of Jerry's eyes, he noticed the salt and pepper shakers on the table. Curious, Wolman placed the salt shaker on top of the pepper container and questioned, "Bruce, what would happen if we put the apartment building on top of the office building?"

The unimpressed architect stared at Wolman's impromptu condiment design. "No, it wouldn't work, plus it would be far too expensive."

Nevertheless, Jerry had a gut feeling. Wolman reminded Graham politely that he was the client and that Graham was the architect. "Bruce," he said, "do me a favor, just check it out." Graham left the meeting disgruntled.

Over the next week, Wolman waited impatiently. He certainly didn't want to refund his million dollar profit nor squander his finest deal. When matters seemed bleakest, the telephone rang. Ted Dailey had arranged a meeting the following day with the architect at the same restaurant.

*****

Bruce Graham greeted Jerry with a hard, gripping handshake and a wide smile. The eager designer immediately placed a sketch of a whopping 120-story building onto a cleared table.

"We have an engineer Fazlur Kahn," he spoke so enthusiastically he salivated. "He's figured out a way to add approximately fifty percent more gross area and go through the clouds!" Graham explained that this young Bangladeshi-American architect had developed a building technique similar to the methods used to build the Eiffel Tower in Paris. The cross bracing system, utilized to reinforce external steel structures in which diagonals intersect, was more economical and didn't require as much steel.

Wolman sat back as Graham likewise enlightened him that Kahn had devised a process to deliver all materials to the higher floors with the use of hydraulic dollies and railroad track-strips positioned along the sides of the skyscraper. Jerry sat listening in amazement.

"Bruce," Wolman interrupted. "This is a lot of information. What does this all mean?"

The architect slammed the table elatedly, "I think we can build the tallest building in the world!"

# John Hancock Center

"It's got to be bold; it's got to have guts; something Chicago will be proud of," Jerry enunciated as if his dream were a holographic vision within his reach. Fazlur Kahn, above whose head Wolman had been gazing in their first meeting, shared Jerry's picturesque dimensional sense of imagination and wonder. As the two young men volleyed ideas, Jerry couldn't help think about his Shenandoah hometowners and what it would mean to them, having one of their own build the world's tallest building. He prized the soon-to-be enhanced vision of Chicago and its reflection upon his birthplace. Jerry's reverent imagination toiled with the notion of calling the building "The Shenandoah."

Prior to authorizing final drawings, Jerry, with Bears owner George Halas in tow, met with Mayor Richard Daley in the latter's sumptuous Chicago office. Daley was a short, heavy-set, seasoned politico who met Halas with outstretched arms. The men initially talked football until the Chicago mayor looked Wolman's way and interrupted, "So what can I do for you?"

Without a word, Wolman gingerly opened his oversized briefcase and took out a three-dimensional cardboard rendering of his mammoth conception.

"Mayor, I'm new in town," Jerry said while unfolding the pop-up emulation of his design. "But I love the city, and I want to do something great here." He placed on Daley's desk the miniature mirror-image of materials to depict what would arise at North Michigan Avenue between East Delaware Place and Chestnut Street.

The mayor brought his fingers to his double-chin and stared at the raised plans of the 120 stories which reached above his thinned hairline. "Go ahead and do it," Daley said with abject awe. "I think it'll be good for the city of Chicago."

Not a week later, in September 1964, Ted Dailey sounded somber on the phone as he related to Wolman that there was bad news: The Federal Aviation Administration had forbid the proposal's height due to regulations concerning airline flight paths. Ten stories had to be cut. Jerry's shoulders sagged, but since there was nothing he could do, he resolved to remain calm and optimistic despite the toppled ten.

Later that month, a phone message arrived from a John Hancock secretary calling for Jerry to meet with Judge Elliott. Wolman conferred with him immediately at Hancock's headquarters in Boston. The judge's lisp was more pronounced than ever when he explained to Jerry the new dilemma.

"My directors have a concern," said the judge. "We want our policy holders to know we're making you the loan for prudent economic reasons, not simply to boast that we're supporting the world's tallest building."

Elliott requested that Jerry remove another ten floors from the building, making it just below the world's tallest, New York's Empire State Building. Jerry's head spun, but his lips uttered that he'd reluctantly review the possibility.

As an aside, Elliott told Wolman off the record about the rivalry that had formed between insurance giants Prudential and John Hancock. Prudential Life Insurance had recently built its skyscraper taller than John Hancock's in Boston. Wolman could sense the edge in Judge Elliott's voice as he conveyed interest in wanting to build higher than the Prudential had in Chicago. Jerry felt buoyed by the swell of bargaining leverage.

The judge proposed in his next swallowed breath, "If you can eliminate ten stories from the top residential floors, we'll attempt to make it up to you somehow."

Wolman wished to build a tower of superlatives and replied by raising the ante.

Jerry countered, "Due to the current plan's increase in gross area over the previous two-building plan, I'll need your 100% loan raised to $72,000,000, plus $750,000 for required expenses of my choosing."

"Name the place the John Hancock Center," the judge's lazy tongue slurped, "and we'll work it out as you suggest."

"Agreed," said Wolman, comforted by the extra funds and the knowledge that the 100 stories, including the planned antennae, would still reach the world's tallest statistical peak.

Bruce Graham of SOM was instructed to proceed with revised drawings. Fazlur Kahn, whose diagonal "X's" were to provide the external steel tubular structure with load-bearing strength, was in the midst of studies and experiments to allay all fears concerning vertical loads and lateral wind loads. Ties, girders and spandrels were maneuvered along the bracing diagonals to be measured against "100-year conditions" for blasts of wind up to 132 miles per hour. Nothing on the top floor could sway more than five to eight inches in any direction. It was noted that there was less velocity of wind in the "Windy City" than in Boston, although Chicago's "lake effect" made it feel that way.

Because the building tapered thinner as it moved upward, ocular tests with eye curvatures were performed to confirm that no one on a top floor could look down and trespass upon the privacy of any other apartment or business on lower floors. Motion perception tests were conducted to assure the elimination of any worries regarding possible "motion sickness."

Wolman met with the architects and engineers weekly through 1964 and early 1965, making essential decisions on every crucial contractor specification, consummating choices for ancillary construction lenders, leasing agents and potential major tenants. He negotiated and sold the rights to power the structure to the electric company for $750,000 so that it could render the building all-electric. Wolman, most importantly, had to choose a General Contractor and envied the work product of Turner Construction Company, but when John Hancock all but insisted that Jerry use Tishman Construction Company, he acceded.

Wolman completed additional boring tests, supplemental wind tunnel tests and oversaw the design of the tracked-hauler dolly used to bring materials upward without a hitch.

By March 1965, all seemed to be in place to construct 46,000 tons of steel, 1,245 panes of glass and 552 crown lights which would be seen from anywhere in Chicago. Complete operational systems, concrete caissons to bedrock, magnificent fixtures and sophisticated equipment were set to transform the components into 100 glorious stories. The structure comprised 1,127 feet skyward, 1,506 feet high with antennae, making it 56 feet taller than even the antennae of the Empire State Building.

The $100 million dollar-valued "vertical city" was to be an engineering miracle that included floors full of retail stores, parking for 1,100 cars, 49 floors of apartments and condos atop 34 floors of commercial offices, a Plaza and an Observatory, top-of-the-skyline restaurants, a 48,000 gallon pool and the fastest elevators in the world to traverse its innards.

The building acquired the nickname "Big John," and was so spectacularly sized at 2,800,000 interior square feet, it required a new zip code all for itself.

When everything was in place to begin, Jerry worried about timing. He knew that birthing "foundation permits" in Chicago could take longer than a human pregnancy, and was likely to be as painful. Delays meant facing dilemmas determinative of time and money. Moreover, Jerry didn't know what notorious political demands, if any, Mayor Daley or bevies of bureaucrats might require in order for him to get an honest count. Jerry wanted to make certain he could proceed with his usual torrid pace. One major problem was Chicago's Building Inspector. There had never before been specifications written for a 100-floor building. With nothing to compare or contrast, Jerry was told it could prolong the acquisition of his building permits up to a year. Jerry hastily met with Mayor Daley for a second meeting.

"Mr. Mayor," Wolman charmed, "I'd like to start our foundations, but the Inspector's Office is reluctant to give us permits. At no cost to the city, I could have my architects and engineers write the safety specifications."

"Wolman," Daley stated with little affect and much esteem, "This shall be a landmark for the city of Chicago." He then assured Jerry that he'd make certain there'd be no further delays.

"You can begin without the permits," allowed the mayor.

Relieved, Wolman knew he could start promptly breaking ground for what he believed was to be an exciting iconic structure: the world's tallest combination residential and commercial building.

Prominent announcements in boldest fonts appeared in Chicago papers, and were screamed aloud by hawkers to sell them, "Eagles Owner Flies High in Chicago."

The Sheraton-Blackstone Hotel hosted the first pre-shovel luncheon. More than five hundred of Illinois Governor Otto Kerner's closest friends shook Wolman's hand redder than the medium rare filet mignon served that day. Jerry Wolman was named Chicago's "first citizen" and the town was abuzz with excitement.

And then a dinner gala was held in Jerry's honor at the Drake Hotel. Seven hundred politicians, John Hancock's upper crust and news media dignitaries surrounded and hugged Wolman and Mayor Daley to congratulate them both. The mayor spoke as if Jerry were royalty, and Wolman reciprocated in kind. Fireworks were omnipresent illuminating the evening's darkness. One sports writer joked above the noise that Wolman's true intent was merely a tall stunt by the Eagles in a deceitful attempt to spy down on Wrigley Field from the 100th floor and infiltrate the Bears' practices.

Wolman and Judge Elliott walked together after the affair, beaming.

"Jerry," inhaled the judge, breathing in the nighttime air, "isn't it wonderful?"

Wolman nodded modestly.

"People will actually reside on top of places people work," pondered Elliott about the novelty. "Can you imagine that?"

"I don't mean to bust your bubble, judge," Wolman countered nostalgically, "but growing up back home our family lived on top of a grocery store."

Judge Elliott placed his arm around Jerry's shoulder and continued down the street.

John Hancock Mutual Life Insurance had just given the high school dropout from Shenandoah the largest single investment sum in its one-hundred-and-three year history.

In May, two months later, construction began.

# Chevy Chase, Maryland — 1965

Jerry had purchased his wife's $200 wedding ring in Shenandoah from "Sol Levit Jewelers" in 1948. He still owed Mr. Levit $100 when he and Anne had picked up the destined hitch-hiker who led them to Washington D.C. With scant financial options, Jerry was forced to return the ring to Levit six months after its purchase. The Shenandoah jeweler, in turn, honorably reimbursed Jerry the much needed $100. The humbling encounter surrounding his wife's wedding ring weighed heavily on his conscience.

Years later in 1964, after having purchased the Eagles, the owner returned home on a frigid February day from a business visit to Atlantic City. That evening he presented an anniversary gift he'd bought for the woman whom he loved most dearly. Jerry placed a $40,000, 8-karat sparkling diamond ring on Anne's bare finger, and softly whispered, "This is to make up for the ring you never had."

Anne thought the gargantuan stone and setting were overwhelmingly beautiful. Her eyes twinkled as she gave her husband an appreciative tight embrace. Throughout the next week, however, Jerry noticed that Anne had never once worn her gift.

"Where's your ring?" he stopped to ask.

Anne answered delicately. "Would you mind if I returned it?" She took her husband's hand and sat him down beside her. "I'll never wear it," she let slip.

Anne Wolman spoke of her neighbors and friends who could never afford to wear such a jewel. Jerry listened to her wise, concerned words and modestly muted tone, and understood why she meant so much to him. The next day, with her spouse's blessing, the ring was returned.

*****

In the early fall of 1965, Jerry bought two hundred acres of superb land in Silver Spring, Maryland, and had Ed Dreyfus design plans for his family's new home. In no time at all, Wolman's architect laid out luxuriant blueprints and sketches that included multiple homes, tennis courts, a swimming pool, a putting green, a baseball diamond and stables for horseback riding.

"Jerry, can I talk to you for a minute?" interjected Anne, sneaking an upside down look at the outlined designs from behind the kitchen table. Wolman followed his wife into the next room.

"I don't need all that," she asserted.

Jerry rubbed his squinting eyes with two index fingers. Anne simply didn't want to leave her neighbors and her friends, and told her husband that the children felt the same way.

"I just need a little more closet space!" she claimed with exasperation.

The next day, Jerry moved the entire family into a hotel while his construction crew bulldozed the Wolman's house. The family remained happily hostage at the Sheraton Hotel for thirty days. After Jerry's workmen had finished all punch lists, the family returned to a new three-story home. Although the house from the outside was only slightly larger than those of their neighbors, inside its rooms were spacious enough for offensive linemen, and consumed with supererogatory closet space.

*****

Jerry always felt it was good luck to pay for Father Hartke's meal when he saw the priest dining at Duke Zeibert's. The two had often dined together and had become friends. Wolman asked Father Hartke at one such repast to do the honors of leading the invocation for the Eagles' pre-game prayer before his players battled the Redskins in D.C.

"If we lose the game," Jerry lightheartedly sanctioned, "I'm hiring Rabbi Ambramowitz!"

One day sitting with Jerry at Duke's, Father Hartke, who had founded the Speech and Drama departments at Catholic University, sounded distressed, seemingly with no appetite.

"They're closing down the Drama Center," he groaned. "The University wishes it could erect a new one, but it doesn't have sufficient funding."

Jerry was overcome with a strong a sense of empathy for the passionate drama professor.

"Father Hartke," he inquired, "if I may ask, how much do they need?"

"One million dollars," griped the priest in a futile, prayerful lilt.

Without hesitation, Jerry pledged a $1,000,000 donation from himself, his friends and subcontractors to Catholic University to build the new Drama Center, assuring its reconstruction.

"I have only one condition," Wolman boyishly grinned as Father Hartke braced himself for Jerry's demand. "It has to be called the Father Hartke Drama Center."

…And a year or so later, it was.

*****

*In 1965 Wolman received a letter from Pope Paul VI, personally thanking him for his attention to Catholic University.*

# THE $100 Million Dollar Fortune

By the latter part of 1965, Jerry Wolman Construction Company was building at the speed of light. While Wolman was laying the foundations at the Hancock Center, he was simultaneously developing over 2,000 apartment units in Maryland and Virginia. He had also just begun projects in areas surrounding Philadelphia, Pennsylvania and Denver, Colorado. Never one to be accused of stagnation, Jerry supplemented his endeavors by commencing a 25-story office skyscraper at 500 North Michigan Avenue in Chicago, three short city blocks from "Big John." All the while, he was intent on entering a successful second season as owner of the Philadelphia Eagles.

Jerry could hardly contain his enthusiasm for "Big John." Like his football team, this was to be a structure that embodied his essence and mirrored his emotions. He monitored a portion of the $750,000 attributed by John Hancock for "extra expenses" to make watches, pins, clothing and other promotional paraphernalia on behalf of the Center. With a seemingly endless supply, Wolman proudly enlivened his friends and business partners with souvenirs of Hancock trappings. New friends and business partners were surfacing everywhere. His list of collaborators was mounting with each new deal born. Approximately thirty persons were silently pampered and partnered by his extravagantly generous business spirit within his largest deals, without any payment, cost or fee. Even the Eagles coaching staff had been cut sweet percentages of the Hancock Center investment pie. Jerry's administrative associates, Foreman and Snider, and friends Teplin and Reines, and a litany of others were experiencing remarkable prosperity with utterly no downside risk. Jerry "the giant-heart," as he was decreed inside the press, wouldn't have had it any other way. Wolman was in his ultra-glorified prime, his heyday of developing dreams. His ability to financially assist and include others became like an adrenaline-rushing drug. Wolman often adhered to his distinct tradition of gifting, originally initiated to reward his attorney and business partner, Earl Foreman. By the mid-1960's, Wolman had gilded the lily, giving out automobiles (mostly new Cadillacs) to over twenty-five people as four-wheeled V-8 tokens of his appreciation. His chrome-laden antics crashed into newspapers' columns where some pundits criticized his gestures as flamboyant folly. When one particular columnist took healthy pot shots at Jerry for the way he was allegedly running his football team, the writer was warned by friends, "Wolman is liable to buy the paper just to fire you."

"Nah," sniped the journalist, "if he buys the paper, I'll show him around the city room and he'll probably buy me a Rolls Royce."

Jerry had reached national celebrity, appearing in news venues across America. After a mere acquaintance of Wolman's had received an Oldsmobile convertible from him as a wedding present, the *New York Post* posed the inevitable unenviable question: "What would Wolman buy a man once he really got to know him?"

*****

Although an eccentric, Wolman was a man with superb fiscal peripheral vision. In 1965, Camden New Jersey's Mayor Alfred Pierce telephoned Jerry to combine efforts, asking the latter to cross over the Ben Franklin Bridge. Pierce showed his neighbor Eagles owner a large area of decrepit, barren land which was owned by the municipality. Standing behind the glass pane of Pierce's office, Jerry looked out upon two hundred and eighty acres of dilapidated waterfront along the Delaware River. Wolman's far-sighted optical vision focused on the possibility of a clear and clean image of booming prosperity.

"We have no plan," uttered the mayor as Jerry's retinas refracted. Wolman adroitly negotiated the purchase of the land from the city for $2,500 per acre after having determined that Pierce was honestly interested in creating a better Camden. Jerry saw waterfront property as prime, gaining value as time moves forward, and time has a way of passing quickly.

"I'd like to build an entirely new city on top of that land," Jerry said with sheer conviction, despite his other most pressing obligations. Recklessly undaunted, he thereafter huddled with his architectural firm, SOM, and together they proposed an entirely innovative conclave: "A City Within A City." Wolman's sights targeted 4,250 housing units and 750,000 square feet of commercial office and retail space along Camden's north shore. His plans portended pristine parks, schools, libraries, religious institutions for all faiths, fire stations, playgrounds and a hotel. 10,000 square feet would be reserved for public use at no cost to coffers of Camden.

Wolman was building one of the tallest structures in the world and now he was attempting to develop and construct an entire city. At the time, the notion of reinventing urban America from scratch was nonexistent. But Jerry thrived on the opportunity for beautifying and uplifting a city. He could strengthen its economy, make a better life for its inhabitants and potentially set an example for the redeployment of funds for development of major inner-cities across the nation.

Word filtered to the local media that Wolman was undertaking a $150,000,000 project to rejuvenate a significant portion of Camden. Everyone in the Delaware Valley and New Jersey took notice and flexed with optimism. Wolman and his group submitted drawings that had erased blight with skillful architectural determination and awaited Camden's City Council for approval.

Wolman's entourage of assets was growing exponentially again. The short baker's dozen of years that had passed since his struggle to obtain his first building loan now seemed like centuries ago. It was difficult not to notice: Jerry Wolman had now amassed a $100,000,000 fortune.

# The Flyers And The Spectrum

The 1930's had been a decade of distant hopes and struggles for Jerry. The 1960's were a period where anything and everything was attainable by him. In his earliest memories from a small coal mining town, young Wolman recalled distinct reveries of his starry-eyed affinity for the big city. When he hitch-hiked to Eagles games or drove his father's truck to Dock Street, the city of Philadelphia, one hundred miles away, presented to him the vast possibilities and aspirations of his adventurous accent on life and livelihood. As a child, he had practically fallen in love with the metropolis which seemed as if it were Shenandoah's big and wonderful brother. Wolman was now determined to tighten his grasp, and prod Philadelphia into becoming a first rate major league sports town.

By March of 1965, after having had twenty-five years of producing a six-team schematic operation, the National Hockey League announced its intention to finally expand. The NHL decided it would double its size and award professional teams to half a dozen cities in specified regions. Those chosen would form a new six-team division and widen the reach of ice hockey in the United States.

Jerry received a call from a faintly familiar, yet difficult to place, name and voice. When Wolman had purchased the Eagles, he used for payment a $5,500,000 dollar draft drawn on Morgan Trust Guarantee. The bank's young, Texas-tall Vice President, Bill Putnam, had handed Jerry the needed check. Jerry recalled Putnam as an avid sports aficionado. He leaned back in his armchair and gladly took the banker's call. Bill told Jerry that he had left Morgan

Guarantee and had thereafter spent a year working for Jack Kent Cooke, a sports mogul in Los Angeles.

"Would you be interested in bringing a hockey team to Philadelphia?" Putnam queried hurriedly.

"Bill, to be honest, I really have no interest in hockey," Jerry responded, but then abruptly caught himself, "But I do really have an interest in buying a team." Wolman conceded that in order for Philadelphia to be considered a major sports city, it needed to be represented by all four big league sports. Jerry flew the thirty-six-year-old former banker from L.A. to Philadelphia and reserved a suitable suite for him at the Bellevue.

Wolman placed his PR director, Hal Freeman, in charge of putting together a neatly wrapped package to be presented to the NHL Board of Governors. The materials prepared by Freeman detailed Philadelphia's superior television and radio markets, its favorable fan interest and the city's statistical attendance figures for its other professional teams.

Wolman understood that the NFL disapproved of owners to acquire majority interests in any other professional team. He decided to bring a handful of loyal people on board to act as his front men on his behalf. Along with Putnam and Freeman, he invited Jerry Schiff, Ed Snider's brother-in-law. Schiff had earlier approached Wolman about getting into the building business, and Jerry had started him in some Pennsylvania construction projects. Wolman also assigned Snider to assist Putnam.

On February 8th, 1966, Wolman, Putnam and Schiff drove to New York City to make their presentation before the NHL Board of Governors. Thirteen other cities were competing, over a few days' time, for the six coveted franchise positions. As is often the case in the world of professional sports, some cities were perceived as frontrunners while others were rumored to be underdogs. Wolman learned with his usual alacrity that Philadelphia was one of those long shots.

Within the selection process, cities in regions of close proximity were pitted against each other. Unfortunately for Philly, it was facing off against the reportedly choice site of Baltimore. Baltimore had top-notch owners who were known to the Board, it had avid fans and boasted excellent facilities to house a rink. On the other hand, Philadelphia had the chilling task of explaining why its most recent hockey team, the 1964 Philadelphia Ramblers of the Eastern League, had fallen through financial ice cracks and dissolved.

Point man Bill Putnam stood behind one podium near Wolman, positioned behind another. They addressed the six member board comprised of the leaders of all existing teams: Detroit, New York, Toronto, Montreal, Chicago and Boston. Bill Putnam led the opening offering for Philadelphia. Seemingly after each key statement Putnam made, the expansion committee responded critically. It discredited his statements, contrasting them unfavorably in support of Baltimore. Then the committee charged that Philadelphia would not be capable of obtaining the necessary support for major league hockey. Wolman interjected hotly to deny the logic of the assessment, citing his Eagles' ample attendance figures as precedent. But it was briskly becoming evident that the puck was sliding towards Baltimore. Time and again, the Board brought up Baltimore's arena facility and belittled the current amphitheater in Philadelphia. The committee emphasized that even Philadelphia's 76ers professional basketball team was required to play more away games that year due to the infrequency of availability at Convention Hall. After a disparaging hour of resistance, the committee called for a short recess. Wolman followed Putman closely into the hallway.

"We've got to do something," the Eagle owner said to the lanky Texan, "we're losing this thing!"

Sweating profusely, Putnam agreed.

Following the break, Bill Jennings of the New York Rangers began speaking candidly to the men representing Philadelphia.

"We have criteria that we're looking for, and to be frank, your city doesn't seem to have them."

"We're the fourth largest television market on the continent!" plugged Putnam.

"That may well be true," replied Jennings, "but our conditions require that an arena holding a minimum of 12,500 seats is a necessity."

Before Jennings could conclude by thanking the Philly group for its time and effort, Wolman reached back to attempt one last slapshot toward the goal.

"If you give us a conditional franchise," Wolman insisted, drawing the attention of the sizeable crowded room, "I'll guarantee that we'll build an arena within one year's time that will seat no less than 15,000 people!"

"That's impossible," uttered Bruce Norris from Detroit.

"No it's not." said Arthur Wirtz, the owner of the Chicago Blackhawks. "He's building a 100-story building in Chicago. If anyone can build a substantial arena in that time," Wirtz pointed his index finger frontward, "it's him."

The room was silenced as the Board began to whisper among themselves. Wolman exhibited a confident smile when he looked directly at Putnam who appeared genuinely ill.

When the committee returned to composure, Jennings cleared his throat and laughed under his breath, "Well then, what more can we ask for?"

Following a few placating pleasantries, the meeting was adjourned.

Absent an appointment, Jerry joined with Mayor Tate the next day at City Hall. First, he buried the hatchet by apologizing for his rude behavior concerning their public stadium squabble; and second, he asked for the mayor's support in building an arena. The former adversaries relinquished their hard feelings noting the need for and benefit of such an entity.

The next day on February 9th, 1966, Philadelphia was awarded a professional hockey franchise. Wolman purchased the team for $2,000,000 by sending a wire for that amount to Bill Putnam in Canada to submit to the NHL offices there; but respecting NFL league policy, he maintained a minority interest of only 22.5% in the hockey club. As usual, he gifted the remainder of the ownership percentages of the hockey team, as well as the new arena at no cost to his many friends and business associates, mainly: Bill Putnam, Jerry Schiff, Hal Freeman and Ed Snider.

Jerry's impetuous and prevailing action to guarantee the construction of a large arena was an additional exorbitantly expensive gesture. By May of 1966, Wolman and the city had reached a unique arrangement. Wolman paid over $8,000,000 to build the sports arena that was soon to be named the "Spectrum." And, with his flair for civic generosity, Jerry announced that under the terms of his agreement, he would *give* the Spectrum upon its completion to the city of Philadelphia in exchange for an exclusive fifty year lease on the land and use of the arena from the municipality. A few weeks later in the beginning of June, construction began.

By mid-1966, Wolman found himself smack dab in the center of a first-rate major league sports city which he was attempting to shape. He owned the Eagles; he was leasing Connie Mack Stadium to the Phillies; he had just founded and purchased the Flyers; and he was about to develop the arena to be home for the 76ers as well as his new ice hockey team.

*****

*"Wolman was a cheerful, charming dreamer who, more than anyone else made Philadelphia a big-league town. The pro franchises were in place before Wolman, but it was he who had the vision to merchandise the NFL before the NFL got around to it. And his was also the spirit behind the building of the Spectrum and the creation of the Flyers."*

-Mike Mallowe, in Philadelphia Magazine's September 1988, Special 80th Anniversary Issue, "Forty Over Eighty," highlighting the top forty people who have left the biggest imprint on the city of Philadelphia over the past eighty years.

Young Wolman (age 9)

Wolman (age 17) in the
Merchant Marines in
Philadelphia, Pa.

Jerry and Anne Wolman on their wedding day at Anne's father's home in Wilkes-Barre, Pa., on February 14th, 1948.

Wolman and partner Nick Basiliko (on left) along with bankers and a mortgage correspondent on the grounds of Summit Hill apartments in 1958.

Wolman with architect Edmund W. Dreyfuss in front of The Executive Building under construction at 15th and L Street NW, Washington, D.C.

New Eagles owner answering
question in his first press
conference.

Wolman with friend,
attorney, and business
partner, Earl Foreman.

"Graduation Day"— April 10th, 1964, at J.W. Cooper High School in Shenandoah, Pa.

Wolman with son Alan.

Wolman with his wife Anne, daughter Helene (age 13) and son Alan (age 11).

Jerry and his lovely wife Anne enjoying their wedding anniversary on February 14, 1965.

Wolman with lifelong
friend and Eagles
equipment manager
Johnny Robel at training
camp in Hershey, Pa.

The owner holding for a hopeful Eagles place kicker at training camp.

Jerry with dear friend Sol Snider.

Eagles head coach Joe Kuharich, team treasurer/vice president Ed Snider and the owner.

Wolman fights a group of hecklers with his wife and daughter in the stands on August 7, 1964, in Hershey, Pa.

Wolman with Robert F. Kennedy before an Eagles-Lions exhibition game at Franklin Field benefiting the JFK Memorial Library Fund on August 23, 1964.

Foreman, Wolman, Sinatra and Taxin at The Old Original Bookbinder's restaurant in Philadelphia.

Wolman and actor Gregory Peck outside the Eagles office building.

The owner with star Eagles Maxie Baughn, Norman Snead, Jim Ringo and Irv Cross with a few members of the Eaglettes inside Philly's office headquarters.

Outside the Eagles offices on 30th and Market Street.

The John Hancock Center Building.

Wolman with members of John Hancock Mutual Life Insurance Company and First
National Bank of Chicago in 1965.

Partial fleet of Wolman's Yellow Cab Companies located on Lackawanna Avenue in
Philadelphia, Pa.

Wolman and Mayor Tate break ground for the Spectrum arena on June 1, 1966. (Photo courtesy of Temple University Libraries, Urban Archives, Philadelphia, Pennsylvania.)

Wolman's and the mayor's associates at the arena's inception.

The Spectrum arena under construction.

Anne Wolman handing the honorary "key to the building" to City Council President Paul D'Ortona beside Spectrum President Hal Freeman.

Wolman next to Johnny Unitas (left) and Colts owner Carroll Rosenbloom (right)
alongside Eagles and Colts star players at the Playoff Bowl on January 7, 1967, in Miami.

Wolman in high spirits following a
victory on the field.

# Mahanoy City

Despite an electrifying year by Eagles wide receiver Pete Retzlaff, who had won the Bert Bell Award for most outstanding player, the Birds finished the 1965 season with a disappointing 5-9 record. More so than ever, Wolman was determined to oversee his football team through a complete rebuilding process. The hungry owner burned to transform the struggling franchise into a feared playoff contender.

In his second year, Wolman had enjoyed the opportunity to become closer with his players; especially his personal favorites: Pete Retzlaff, Jim Ringo, Irv Cross and Ollie Matson of the Eagles convocation. As he had reacted in his early construction years treating his sub-contractors as family members, Jerry's newest found family was tailored in green jerseys. Publicly, Jerry gained most attention by donning sweat pants, tying his cleated sneakers' laces and participating in practices on the field. However, Wolman's relationships with his players off the field were furtively more extraordinary.

A professional athlete was by no means being paid a millionaire's salary in the mid-1960's. Therefore Wolman began assisting his players on occasion in businesses to supplement their incomes. He did not hesitate to offer star Eagles defensive back Irv Cross support for a real estate deal he coveted. Once, he even advanced Eagles safety Glenn Glass the needed funds to start a ski resort in Gatlinburg, Tennessee. Wolman stinted with no player or anyone on his staff from bottom to top. When he had learned that Leo Carlin, a young assistant in the Eagles ticket office was unable to get to Jerry's son's Bar Mitzvah on time in Washington D.C., Wolman called his employee and assured Leo of the needed transportation. Wolman flew Carlin and his wife in his plane and provided a limousine to take the couple to the services and celebration in style.

Wolman's "open door" policy epitomized the definition of the term "players' owner." Jerry listened intently in his office for hours on end as players or personnel in one sort of trouble or another sought advice on topics involving business as well as their marital, personal and emotional health.

Wolman was unfailingly empathetic and wounded after Coach Kuharich traded and/or cut players. After lineman John Myers had been traded, Jerry felt so badly, he stopped by to personally bid him good luck and farewell. When John's wife opened the front door of her home, she saw the Eagles owner standing on her steps with a handful of boxes.

"I'm sorry, what are *you* doing here?" the player's befuddled wife asked.

"I feel terribly that your husband was traded," Jerry answered, "so I came by to help you move."

And he did.

Wolman, after having begun the John Hancock Center, never felt so deeply involved with and devoted to another transaction revolving around real estate. The deals dallied before him seemed more or less like buying and selling produce. The Eagles football franchise, on the other hand, was imbedded in his bones. He prized his team above all of his assets and believed he was destined to nestle within its confines for as long as he lived.

*****

Earl Foreman and his brother-in-law Ed Snider were Wolman's right and left arms, assisting him in crafting all of his decisions. The former was Jerry's most trusted longtime counselor; the latter was a go-getting son of an old-time friend upon whose business acumen and loyalty he depended. The triumvirate formed a chain of expertise and confidence.

With the klieg lights shining on the charismatic owner, Jerry reached out to acknowledge the two men publicly in the press and at every function they attended. He genuinely wanted his comrades to feel as nourished by success as he. When Wolman attended league meetings for owners at resorts in Miami, Palm Springs and Hawaii, he always invited Foreman and Snider and their families. Other owners in the league were infrequently accompanied by their front office staff, associates and family members. But Wolman was distinctively accommodating. Jerry thought it was a privilege to have everyone together. Wives and children were as inseparable as the owners.

*****

While traveling from city to city on business trips with Eagles Vice President Ed Snider, Jerry would bend his ears and warm his heart with stories about the people of Shenandoah. Without fail, wherever they were, someone always had a relative in or a relation to Shenandoah. In jest, Ed played upon Jerry's recounting, to introduce himself in Jerry's presence as a native son of Mahanoy City, a Pennsylvania coal town not four miles from Jerry's home. Ed made sure to put the proper emphasis on the "HA" in Mahanoy.

A few years prior, Snider had been beside Wolman riding through Shenandoah's main streets on Jerry's motorcade where the crowd's fervor and support had been unconditional. Therefore, Jerry hatched an idea following the Variety Club's "Heart of Gold Award," a fifteen-hundred-guest extravaganza honoring him. He began to concoct an event which parlayed with the faux birthplace invented by Snider's Mahanoy white fib.

"If Ed was telling people he was from Mahanoy City, Pennsylvania," thought Jerry plotting to himself, "then we better make it official." Wolman, with the help of Eagles promotions maven Gene Kilroy, organized an historic event for Mahanoy City. Eight hundred rollicking people geared up to encourage and honor Ed Snider for all his efforts as Eagles Vice President and his assistance with launching the soon-to-be-named hockey team, the Philadelphia Flyers.

On May 22nd, 1966, a gala Schuylkill County sports banquet was held at the Lakewood Ballroom. Wolman was as happy as a miner striking gold as he watched Ed Snider occupying the place of honor at the head table. Following the musical mastery of the 112-piece Mahanoy Area band, Snider received a roaring standing ovation from the assemblage of the borough's tickled Eagle-green Pennsylvanians.

Adopted as "Native Son" by Mahanoy City Citizens, Ed was given the key to the city. During the ovation, Jerry caught the attention of Sol, Ed's father, who silently winked at Wolman and his imaginative marketing.

"Jerry Wolman is one heck of a guy," Ed began, "and I love him very dearly." When concluding, Snider spoke directly to the high school seniors present. He closed his rabble-rousing rhetoric by surmising that since he was now an adopted citizen of Mahanoy City, he pledged with vigor, "We're going to beat Shenandoah in football this year!" And with that popular prediction, the crowd rallied riotously.

Following a short speech by Coach Kuharich, Wolman took to the center of the podium. Clearing his throat, Jerry opened by jokingly chiding Snider for not bearing any resemblance to a coal miner. Then the owner unexpectedly spoke seriously and from his heart.

"This is indeed one of the happiest moments of my life to see you good folks of Mahanoy City honoring Ed Snider. There is no man that you can count on more when the chips are down." Walking tall back to his seat, Jerry could see the joy on Ed's face. All the money in the world could not buy or replace it.

# The Caisson Failure

Wolman eagerly looked forward to arriving at training camp in the summer of 1966 for the Birds' most anticipated and potentially promising season. The team had just undergone what it considered to be its finest draft and off-season under its auspicious owner's regime. Players were now getting acclimated to Kuharich's schemes and practice style. The explosive legs of Timmy Brown were primed for take-off and a young tackle Bob Brown was developing into a real superstar on the line.

By July of '66, Wolman had diversified his holdings beyond the spheres of real estate and professional sports. Continuing his persistently behavioral buying spree, Jerry had purchased The Yellow Cab Companies of Philadelphia and Camden for $7,000,000. The second largest cab carriers in the nation, The Yellow Cab Companies retained 5,200 employees and utilized 1,500 taxis. Its 4,750 drivers steered a cash flow of $1,000,000 per year. Wolman also purchased the Yellow Limousine Service, Inc.

Although the buyer-tycoon was carving larger and more varied pieces of the American Dream for himself and others, his passion was to pursue the game of football. There seemed to be little challenge left for completing new buildings. The past two years' conceptualizing the development of "Big John" had been like climbing the tallest pinnacle of the highest mountain. He had reached a decision that once the Hancock Center was completed, he'd devote full time and all his concentration on the Eagles. Wolman had made up his mind: After having fulfilled every effort toward the emergence of countless apartments and office buildings over a decade's time, his colossal Hancock Center would be the last major edifice.

Jerry was flying once a week or more to Chicago to stay current with the grueling growth of the Center. After a year of burying nearly three hundred concrete foundation caissons, many six feet in diameter, almost two hundred feet to bedrock (much deeper than anyone had expected), the blossoming building had ascended approximately one-fifth of the way up. It was progressing rapidly ahead of schedule. Standing apart from the sea of two thousand workmen on the job, Wolman couldn't believe how smoothly their efforts were moving his creation forward and upward.

One August morning, while seated behind his desk in his D.C. construction office at 8:30 a.m., Jerry received a telephone call from Ted Dailey. His friend, and now one of Jerry's many donee-partners of the Hancock Center, was panicked and spoke with a noticeably truncated voice.

"Jerry, we've got a big problem," Ted's vocal chords reverberated with tremors, "a caisson failed; they said it moved or settled..."

Wolman's entire body seemed to shrink as his eyebrows curled below the gathering creases of his forehead. Attempting to gain some sense of cognition, he quickly scrambled through his office filing drawers for the foundation's footing plans, hoping that the issue was not a serious one. The builder quickly called Tishman's foreman and anyone else on the site he could reach. Jerry was somewhat relieved that the breakdown seemed to have transpired near the corner of the building and appeared to be slight. At the very, very worst, Wolman estimated that he'd simply have to dig down alongside the failed caisson and re-strengthen it. He let out a sigh and counted his blessings. The news was horrible, but the end of the world was far from near. No fix would be cheap, but Wolman's past experiences and embedded ego subtly reminded him it was only money.

Jerry called Ted back to lessen his partner's concerns. But Dailey stammered and ranted about the construction crews, "Those stupid sons of..."

"Ted," Jerry interrupted the firestorm, "how bad can it be?"

Dailey pleaded with his friend to come to Chicago immediately.

*****

Late that evening, Jerry customarily checked into his room at the Continental Hotel in Chicago without stopping to see his building, and got one last night of good, sound sleep.

By the time he arrived on the site early the next morning, all hell had broken loose. Wolman could sense in the unhealthy humidity that something far more catastrophic was unraveling. He observed hundreds of workmen standing around swiping away at their August perspiration. They all stared grimly at him as he warily made his way through the maze of men. Jerry approached the project's building inspector who was listening to and blanching from the shouts of the short, slim, lead engineer. Fazlur Kahn had been presiding over a demanding and damning one-sided exchange with the inspector. The boisterously agitated engineer had viewed the "moving" caisson first-hand. It was impossible, he described for all to hear, for a six foot circular solid concrete shaft, resting on bedrock two hundred feet deep, to have settled almost an inch into the ground's soil, which it definitely had. Khan insisted that drastic cautionary measures be taken at once.

Jerry could discern "We've just got to!" from Kahn's troubled fast-moving mouth. Wolman came closer to stand opposite him.

"Lives are at stake!" the engineer verbally clobbered him. Kahn felt strongly that even an infinitesimal foundation footing glitch could serve as a harbinger of great danger that could potentially jeopardize people's lives.

Jerry watched as Kahn shook his head and crossed his hands high in the air, waiving his open palms back and forth like a referee stopping a prizefight. The building's owner stood by helplessly atop cluttered rubble as the rising sun glowered. Kahn decreed definitively, "We're shutting it down!"

And with those four words, in that instant, Wolman's visions and dreams of building the world's grandest vertical community had been temporarily cut short, to the quick.

The following day, three-inch tall headlines scoured the front pages of newspapers across the country, accentuating "CAISSON FAILURE AT THE HANCOCK CENTER" like terrifying words splattered across a horror movie marquee.

# THE QUANDARY

**W**ithin hours of newspapers hitting people's doorsteps, Wolman received a call in Chicago from the manager of his personal local bank, American National Bank of Maryland.

"Jerry, what's going on over there?" tepidly questioned the money lender's head man. "The folks here are a little worried."

"Give it a few days," assured Wolman, "we'll figure it out by the end of the week."

But after a few days' study, nobody could as yet understand the underlying root of the predicament.

More calls began pouring in for Jerry, each nervously wanting confirmation and assurances that no assets were in jeopardy. Wolman began receiving letters, memos and telegrams from banks, mortgage lenders and subcontractors seeking to protect their respective monetary interests. Pressure mounted and encircled the tarnished Boy Wonder from every direction. Young Claire was inundated at the Washington construction office, deluged by waves of calls from local banks.

Wolman had been the most favored client of Morgan Guarantee and Trust Company. He had purchased the Philadelphia Eagles with a check from a Morgan Guarantee credit line, and had later accomplished the purchase of the Philadelphia Flyers in a similar transaction. Whenever he had visited the bank, its Vice President, H. Livingston Schwartz would fawn over Jerry, gushing in friendliness and with familiarity by referring to the millionaire builder only by his first name. Even if Schwartz were in the midst of an ongoing meeting, any time the banker saw or was advised of the presence of the Eagles owner at Morgan's offices, he'd run out of his conference to pump Wolman's hand with both of his.

Forty-eight hours following the chilling headlines denoting "Big John's" stoppage, Jerry received a formal letter from H. Livingston Schwartz of Morgan Guarantee and Trust Company. It began:

"Dear *Mr. Wolman*: We hereby make demand for payment in full of your outstanding indebtedness no later than 5:00 p.m. on Friday."

Jerry was stunned and cross as he crumpled the paper and threw it down on his desk. Friday was three days away.

Despite his "backers'" nervousness and legal posturing, Wolman's outlook on the construction quandary remained steadfast and optimistic. His plan was to take control of the puzzling event and coordinate the efforts of everyone on his team in order to get the matter fixed.

At sunrise the next morning on the site's leveled ground, Jerry gathered his architects, engineers and subcontractors around him in a close elliptical oval as if they were a sundial.

Unfortunately, no one could identify the actual cause of the sinking setback. Each participant had his or her own ideas how to proceed. They all agreed upon, however, that the dilemma in the corner caisson was an isolated freak anomaly; everyone, that is, but Fazlur Kahn. The fastidiously mustached, careful structural engineer demanded that a thorough safety inspection of *all* the caissons be made, requiring the invasive use of a specifically designed giant laser drill manufactured and stationed in Canada. Not only did the investigative equipment cost its user $10,000 per diem, but it would also take at least three weeks before the gigantic apparatus arrived on the scene.

Wolman's career had been predicated on constant coordination and continuous speed. Mired in demand-plagued notices augmenting the temperature in what had become a financial furnace, the delay was an expensive, explosive disaster. He agonized as he waited three coin-clawing weeks.

No one could ever have foreseen how severe the carnage was to be. Once the drilling began on the faulty corner caisson, a ruinous fourteen foot void in the concrete had been discovered almost immediately. The laser drill bore through the top portion of the shaft so easily after just twenty to thirty feet down that it strongly suggested to the engineers the existence of a vacuum of empty airspace beneath the surface. After the laser drill dug deep into another sizeable caisson founded on bedrock, the team discovered that the same infiltration of air and soil had occurred. They continued to drill others randomly and devised a wave-length detector to lower through the lasered shoots to determine inconsistencies in the concrete's solidity. Twenty-six of the fifty-seven deepest caisson shafts failed the testing. Over the next two months, to everyone's chagrin, the examinations revealed that each foundation-bearing shaft was similarly flawed. Tens and hundreds of feet beneath the soil's surface, gaping crevices of empty space were filling with mushed debris.

A devastated Dailey, who beforehand had quit his job with Advance Mortgage to concentrate as a partner on the Center, wearily explained to Jerry what had been determined to have occurred. Over the many months that the cavernous caissons had been drilled and filled with concrete, an egregious miscalculation had taken place.

Working with unprecedented massively deep foundations, SOM engineers devised an innovative method of pouring concrete in stages. The end result was tragic. Instead of using one long steel lining to act as a shell to contain all of the poured concrete, the engineers designed the use of a smaller steel "sleeve" approximately twenty feet long and six feet in diameter. Not only would the smaller casings be easier to maneuver, they would spare the project over $1,000,000 in steel tubing.

After an augur had driven downward almost two hundred feet and had cleared a wide circular hole to bedrock, the steel "sleeve" casing was then lowered to the bottom. Cement was thereafter poured, filling the casing to its top. When the cement was thought to have dried, the lining was pulled up about seventeen to eighteen feet and filled again. When that batch of cement had dried, the "sleeve" was once again raised another seventeen or eighteen feet to be filled with cement; and so on and so on, until the casing had been fully retrieved at ground level. Upon completion, the process was to have left a solid shaft of concrete from top to bottom.

But over the course of pouring, the "sleeves" had evidently

been pulled too quickly before the concrete had had opportunity to dry. By doing so, the steel casings had extracted portions of concrete as they were being intermittently raised, thus causing gaps beneath the surface. The misapplication of the shorter casings had doomed the caissons to desuetude.

Fazlur Kahn dictatorially declared, "Every caisson has to come out!"

Wolman's blood boiled at the thought. By ordering the removal of every caisson, Kahn rendered Jerry speechless and dizzy, with buckling knees. Teary-eyed, he watched for days as cranes lifted "Big-John's" girders, denuding it of approximately twenty trussed stories. One million man-hours of work were vanishing minute by excruciating minute, piece by piece.

Everything changed. As Fazlur Kahn prepared new specifications to remove and replace the caisson structures from scratch, Jerry attempted to glue and paste everything and everyone together. The scenario, however, of potential major legal claims and allegations, caused Wolman's construction team to grow eerily cold and distant toward him. Nobody would discuss anything with Jerry, and if someone inadvertently did, the conversing was guarded and terse. Tishman, the general contractor, along with Case Foundation, Tishman's sub-contractor which had poured the concrete, quietly withdrew from the ken of the building's owner. It was clear to Jerry that people had been forewarned and instructed not to speak to him. A miasma of cataclysmic legal magnitude was gaining momentum. Soon there was no one left who had not scrambled to cover his hide. Finger-pointing was now the prevalent body-language. All eyes peered accusingly at the person appointed "scapegoat" solely because his signature matched that of the man who'd approved the final design plans: Jerry Wolman, the owner.

Remediation would require three shifts of workmen four months and four days to re-insert new foundation-caissons so that the building could be borne again. It was unclear whether the man who had conceived "Big John" would still be present to watch his building grow up.

# Losing "Big John"

An unusually large albatross accompanied by bands of buzzards were hovering overhead when Wolman's financial problems began to stumble into quicksand. Making matters even worse, he had used his own cash and personal lines of credit to commence the Center's construction with his usual inexorable appetite to get the promptest start, to stay well ahead of schedule and to complete in mind-boggling speed. That mindset tic coupled with his torrid time-line aptitude had always worked without fail in the past and never without huge returns.

Based on the strength of the primary Hancock permanent loan, he had gone to a handful of banks in Chicago and New York to arrange for a $72,000,000 construction loan. Once he had commitments upon which to reliably depend, he knew it would still take a few months of paperwork and formalities before he could draw down on them. But rather than wait, since time is money, his judgment was to forge ahead using funds from his own deep pockets. Wolman anticipated that personally priming the job's propulsion would be temporary in the short run and phenomenally lucrative in the long. This infallible practice had been used by him to catapult profits on dozens of previous endeavors.

However, the moment it had been determined that the caisson failures were pervasive, the availability of the flow of money screeched to a halt. No longer would either John Hancock or the intermediary banks allow Wolman to make use of the loans to which they had committed. They claimed his default, rendering him unable to recoup his gambled out-of-pocket advances.

Prior to the corner caisson's sinking an infinite inch, Wolman had paid over $3,000,000 to SOM architects and engineers, plus complementary fees for various studies with enormous operating expenditures. He had dutifully disbursed $15,000,000 for foundations, steel and construction for twenty built floors. Furthermore, he had laid out a subsequent $3,000,000 to drill, remove, repair and/or replace the faulty cement shafts. His bank accounts had been depleted to bedrock and all but echoed in hollowness. His liquidity had become momentarily paltry and parched. But he remained intrepid in his belief that he could forestall doom by wagering his fountain of other real estate assets with flowing chips, all in the black.

He looked to squeeze the equity in his construction complex enterprises to quench the thirst of his circling creditors. But one-third of his real estate developments at that particular time were actively, aggressively and concurrently being built. There were nearly 3,000 apartment units under construction, therefore not many had yet been completed or fully rented.

With each passing day, the buzzing overhead sounded louder and nearer. Wolman no longer had the ammunition of money to swat the debt-demons away. Scattered on sites along the mid-Atlantic seaboard, his general contractors and their subcontractors began to slowly simmer their efforts, fearing that they'd never be paid. Wolman's perfect synergy of a well-oiled building machine was out of fuel and all but irreparably sputtering. No one wished to wait for money owed. His reputation with banks, lenders and corps of workers was toppling.

By the late fall of 1966, near Thanksgiving, creditors had succeeded in filing their liens against the Hancock Center property. Demands for payments were being thrown like darts directed precisely at a bulls-eye on Jerry's chest covering his heart. Wolman had simply undertaken too much at the same time. Hopeful for a way out, he futilely attempted to shuffle his empire's financial cards in Chicago's gusts of wind.

Wolman refused to surrender without a ferocious fight. First, he jabbed at clearing away his worst problem assets in a suddenly deteriorating real estate market. Notwithstanding, concerned for the welfare of his twenty-five partners who had ownership in his apartment properties, Wolman organized a meeting in the Eagles' offices to discuss his plans to attempt to resolve his predicaments. Jerry opened the meeting by informing all concerned that they could be made whole. He offered each partner whatever percentage interest of fair market value that partner had been given, payable in cash. Wolman's conscience wouldn't allow or accept anything otherwise. By buying everyone's position, his supposed missteps and problems would no longer be theirs. After having undertaken to salvage his associates by agreeing to liquidate almost eighty percent of his construction portfolio, he rallied around a plan to seek buyers for his holdings before being forced into a formal and final foreclosed posture. He circled his wallet and his wagons in a frenzy, and contracted to finalize his redemption at the settlement of his humongous real estate divestment.

Desperately, Wolman raced throughout the country trying to close transactions in order to augment his cash. What he soon discovered was that everyone smelled the blood of his need for transfusions of dollars. Without exception, all buying entities offered only half-value prices for what Wolman's bleeding real estate holdings were actually worth. Finally, after having traveled tirelessly in November for two fortnights from city to city, day after day, he was constrained to make "Black Friday" bargain deals to sell a majority of his apartment buildings. What had taken him thirteen years to build included 10,000 apartment units, a third of which were a recent batch still under construction. Their total appraised value had been set at $135,000,000 earlier that year. By the close of November in 1966, Wolman sold almost his entire lot of labor for $99,375,000 in one drooping fell swoop. He hardly saw any of that money as the sum went directly to creditors at settlement to close and successfully stave off foreclosures. Having been forced to accept seventy-five percent of the properties' depressed value, and having been required to appease his partners in the ventures and miscellaneous creditors, Wolman found himself still $10,000,000 in the red.

The moment construction had been stopped on the Hancock Center, Wolman's destiny had been disabled. He was no longer cash-capable to finalize his lists of apartment units. Camden's "City Within a City" project evaporated. His charitable efforts to build Catholic University's Drama Center stalled amid construction and had to be completed despite his uncompleted pledge. Wolman's real estate holdings had been fumbled and pounced upon by others. However, he still maintained valuable ownership interests in The Hancock Center, The Yellow Cab Companies, Connie Mack Stadium, The Philadelphia Flyers, The Spectrum Arena and above all, his most prized possession that defined his very being: The Philadelphia Eagles.

John Hancock, once enthusiastically dedicated to magnificent architectural innovation, had all but surrendered to the tragedy. The Hancock group, along with the architects and engineers froze in place, collapsing and frightened to take any action even in the face of Jerry's risk-his-riches remedial efforts. Bob Jordan, who was assigned to the project by Hancock, fearing the flat-lining fate of his own employment, began dictating terms wildly of what had to be done. No one claimed accountability and inaction filtered any vortex of hope. A fractured bureaucratic mess ensued enslaving all rational thought. Clearly the saga was becoming a tremendous public embarrassment to the sensitivities of John Hancock, whose name was shared with the struggling building's. Privately, the Hancock Board felt it most prudent to cut ties and association with the beleaguered builder.

Demolishing the building permanently would have meant even more humiliation for the insurance giant. Instead, Hancock's upper echelon decided to make a deal with Wolman to root him out. Still severely in the hole and in the epicenter of the fight for his livelihood, Wolman sold whatever rights he held in the Hancock Center back to Hancock for $5,500,000 above its original loan. As he accepted the deal, he was gone. With sizeable liens still outstanding and executable on the Hancock property, Wolman was unable to keep almost any of Hancock's buyout payment. It was devoured by his creditors to clear title.

Bowed and crawling away from the Center was devastation personified. Jerry knew he had put together one of the greatest deals in the history of American real estate. He had received the largest single loan by John Hancock Mutual Life Insurance Company and ironically had never touched a nickel of it. He stepped away broken and almost insolvent, but ready to battle with determination and optimism via the force of his ownership interests in his sports-related holdings.

He had to keep his spirit alive for whatever maneuvers he could manage to save what was left: most importantly his treasured Philadelphia Eagles.

# Mixed Emotions

Paradoxically for Jerry, the worst agitation from financial setbacks and collapses was combined with culminating successes for his Eagles. The 1966 season had evolved into a series of victories for the high-flying Philadelphia football franchise. After having initially lost three out of their first five games, the team caught on-field fire just before mid-season, winning a blistering seven out of its final nine contests. The owner, on the other hand, was living a personal nightmare off the field during all phases of play. Unable to feel like a winner, he was enduring his own hard-hitting battle against financial anguish. By the time his Eagles had won its final four games of the season, he had reached his own monetary end zone in Chicago.

As owner, a winning team had been his only goal. All the football diehard had ever hoped for and wanted was victory, but now Jerry was sorely reminded of what he had so freely taken for granted: his financial health. Fearing that the extent of his troubles would leak out to the press, Wolman exhibited jolly cheerfulness and dimpled smiles at games, and anywhere near the press box. His external visage attempted to mimic a confident, carefree cockiness. Underneath this outward facade, he was all but overwhelmed with anxiety and trepidation.

Following the Philadelphia's breakaway 9-5 season, the Eagles marched with enthusiasm to the Playoff Bowl in Miami. Gaining nation-wide attention as a franchise-on-the-rise, Wolman's Eagles squared off against the celebrated and storied Baltimore Colts. Before the game, Jerry sauntered squeamishly onto the field to shake the certain-to-be Hall of Fame hands of quarterback legend, fellow Pennsylvanian Johnny Unitas. What would truly have been a thrill for Jerry was marred by bolting waves of voltage-driven panic attacks.

Instead of reveling in the biggest event of his career as owner, Wolman remained seated during the Bowl game, attempting to ward off waves of worry and concealment of his financial tribulations. He hardly noticed when Baltimore running back Tom Matte scored the winning Colts touchdown with fourteen seconds remaining in the game, capping a come-from-behind playoff victory over his Eagles. The season had ended, but the future seemed bright for a team heading steadily on a path to heralded wins. On the flight home to Philadelphia, Jerry reflected intensely above the sounds of some snoring players and both airplane engines.

With the advent of 1967, the Hancock Center and its ancillary tremors in tow behind him, the tycoon in trouble had to strategize to re-equip his moneybags and his reputation for infallibility. He desperately needed to come up with $10,000,000. The sands in Wolman's fairy-tale hour glass were filtering down with gravity.

*****

Jerry still owned a handful of large apartment complex developments that he hadn't sold in the November transaction. He began the year seeking buoyant back-up cash by attempting to make a few more sales to a number of investors and banks in order to stay afloat. He worked arduously, with all his bearing, to get loans for the continued production of the construction matters he had in progress, which had been now labeled "in limbo." But horrible timing tempered and then foiled his chances. Unfortunately, the real estate market was falling downward on top of his head like piercing hail. Due to the severe climate conditions, the market values of his properties were plummeting perilously below that of his considerable mortgages. The burden of taxes, accruing interest, insurance costs, and wear and tear expenses, dashed every ounce of optimism. Large projects like the massive Philly sports arena were underway in construction, and many other apartment ventures were likewise under development. Wolman was trapped, caught in the headlights of his own bulldozers. His only hope was to wait out the downturn, but time was not on his side. The events of Chicago had damaged his reputation, and an uneasy cluster of three hundred impatient creditors would not wait much longer.

Jerry concentrated on using his remaining properties simply as collateral for additional loans. But near record high interest rates made doing so unobtainable for him. Trying to negotiate refinancing on his buildings and sports ownership interests became grueling and futile. Painfully reminded of his days starting out in the building business, he faced rejection upon rejection. Credit had been shut off at the nozzle of all banks whose hoses he attempted to yank.

Working late through the night, the forty-year-old magnate slept in his office for months while running around during the days chasing any and all potential lenders. Feeling as if he'd been turned down by every single loan officer in the country, one day in the spring of 1967, Jerry received a phone call from Ted Dailey. "I've got people overseas who are looking to make a deal," Dailey blurted.

From his days with Rouse Company and Advance Mortgage, Ted Dailey had channeled connections all over the world. He was familiar with Dr. Josef Seiler, an international broker who represented wealthy Middle Eastern contacts. Ted was able to reconnect and stay in touch with Seiler following Wolman's disentanglement in Chicago.

"They're a group of Kuwaiti businessmen. It's Arab oil money, and they've got barrels of it," Ted explained to Jerry. "Also," he added curiously, "they're extremely interested in hockey."

First Dailey traveled overseas to feel out the foreign financiers to see if he could mold minds around a fully wrapped and bowed package of Jerry's equities. Within a week of his departure, Dailey contacted Wolman euphorically, "I think we've got something here!" Ted was overjoyed to share with Jerry his lifesaving news: an amenable deal involving tens of millions of dollars was on the table.

# Paris - 1967

O n the home front, Jerry sensed that he needed to cleanse his holdings by clearing out all of his partners in order to move more freely. In preparing to receive the foreign financing now in the pipeline, Wolman first set out to meet with over a dozen of his own participant owners to offer them compensation for their interests which they had been given during Wolman's string of flourishing successes.

Wolman was vehemently insistent upon protecting everyone, even if none had ever contributed a penny. For the next few weeks, Jerry went to all parties involved and met with each personally to discuss making them whole. Over the past several months, he had clawed and struggled to stave off bankruptcy. In the back of his mind, a creditors-forced bankruptcy could come at any moment in the absence of financing overseas. In such event, Wolman had been advised those who had been included in any of his deals would lose all of their interests and suffer the consequences. Jerry was unwilling to take his friends down with him in this shared looming scenario. Therefore, a proposed arrangement was offered to each shareholder. To a man, they all appeared appreciative and relieved.

Knowing the foreign suitors held particular interest in the hockey club, Wolman gave astute attention to those holding equity or options with the recently named "Philadelphia Flyers." At the time, the team had yet to play a single professional game.

Jerry approached his hockey-holding partners for their approval. He made acceptable arrangements with his friends, employees, coaches and even his brother Manny. He then met with the team's core interest holders: Putnam, followed by Schiff, Freeman and Snider. In order to obtain clear title to his hockey team's assets, Wolman offered Bill Putnam $1,000,000 to be paid out of the proceeds of his anticipated designed foreign deal. Similarly, Jerry prearranged for a $1,000,000 package for Ed Snider in exchange for Ed's return of previously obtained shares from Jerry's deals, except with regard to the Eagles (for which Snider held a minor interest). Jerry assured Ed, "This will straighten everything out; it will save me and we'll have the Eagles forever." All of the men agreed to the outlined plans.

Many of the gentlemen seemed ecstatic. Jerry even promised the men he'd bring them back in one capacity or another after he put his own fires out. He'd be able to refinance all his assets and get a clean first mortgage on all of his properties as a whole suite.

Weeks later as matters progressed, Ted called Jerry long distance to advise him that negotiations were solidifying. "I need you to come over here!"

Wolman was thrilled, though apprehensive. He had heard rumors about foreign businessmen. Jerry was warned of their unscrupulous and tightfisted, close-to-the-vest tactics. Moreover, he was also uneasy about being a Jew dealing with Arabs. Egypt and Syria, in May 1967, had given signals that an attack on Israel was forthcoming. Border clashes had increased along the Golan Heights, and Syria had mobilized its forces. Anti-Israeli rhetoric from Cairo, Baghdad and Jordan demanded the total destruction of Israel. Meanwhile, Israel had also mobilized to launch pre-emptive attacks along the Sinai Peninsula and the Gaza Strip. On June 5th, 1967 the Six Days' War began, and ended on June 10th. Jerry was not without legitimate concerns over how things might play out when he flew to Paris that July to confer and do business. Ted Dailey was advised by Seiler to ask that Jerry neither speak to nor introduce himself to anyone.

Wolman arrived at the Lancaster Hotel on Rue de Berri, a petite promenade to the Champs-Elysees. Sumptuously luxurious, the Parisian townhouse had only twelve or so grand chambers. It provided the softest silk pillows, giant beds and servants to match every whim with satisfaction. Dinner was at a restaurant called Zavan's. There, Wolman was encouraged by eight elegantly dressed Arab courtiers in suits, reviewing the American's, as Wolman was called, transactional package. Ayub Malik, a heavy-set bearded Arab gentleman had led the group from Kuwait. Josef Seiler was also present at the table. Quickly, their conversation turned to mention of a Prince from Dubai.

"We've talked to the Prince, and he loves your hockey club," said Malik. As the discussion evolved, the representatives spoke of bringing a respected associate in Canada to head and run the hockey team. After having monitored months of hopeless rejection, Jerry's pulse was reawakening with the pounding beat of a deal that was clearly being realized in the Paris night.

The Kuwaiti businessmen asked a seemingly never-ending amount of intricate questions. Jerry answered each while describing every asset from the paper entrails within a suitcase overflowing with receipts and figures. He knew his numbers, mortgages, rates, pre-payment penalties, amortization schedules and default provisions. The authorized representatives of the Prince were utterly impressed. And so was Wolman. These men were serious, smart and shrewd professionals. A deal was nearly set in stone after the last course had been served. However, the Kuwaitis required signed papers from all of the American's partners. In exchange for a $45,000,000 refinancing loan to cover all of Wolman's properties and interests, the foreign representatives required the acquisition of the hockey club. The loan was to be structured so that Wolman would have ample cash flow to service the new indebtedness. The debt was to be secured by his remaining properties. The American's Eagles stock would also be proffered and pledged as security. The proposed sum would save Wolman. The money mentioned was enough principal to clear his debts to all mortgage holders and other creditors. By selling the Flyers and refinancing, Jerry could hold the rest of his empire intact. Most importantly, the Eagles were his to keep. The hard luck developer was saturated with relief.

That morning at 2:00 a.m. inside Zavan's, after the Arabs had left for their hotel, an intoxicated Wolman celebrated with Ted Dailey. Upon leaving, Jerry giddily gave the band a generous tip and asked the musicians, along with their instruments, to follow them to their hotel. On the streets of Paris, for six blocks in the middle of the morn, the band played upbeat tunes of celebration behind the two jubilant Americans as they passed through the Arc de Triomphe.

Thereafter, the group met four times in the next two days to exchange documentation. The internationals wined and dined Jerry and Ted with the utmost class. Wolman had been treated with wonderful hospitality, and for the first time in a decade, he had never touched a check.

Jerry flew home that July on cloud nine.

# Betrayal

The following week, Wolman was airborne again to Geneva, Switzerland for what was described to him as a "social affair" with the Kuwaiti investment group. Once there, Dailey and Wolman drove into a gated private property preceded by a breathtaking one-mile stretch of paved road. Groomed trees lined the driveway on both sides as if standing at attention, leading up to what appeared to be a large, opulent stone house. The seeming home amended its identity to become a restaurant inside. The lavish dining hall was encased by giant translucent glass windows. The twosome approached nearly twenty men seated at a sixty foot white-clothed table. Wolman was all smiles, but followed instructions to be cautious with any personal pleasantries.

Looking around the extravagantly set room, Jerry couldn't believe how far away he was from his Pennsylvanian coal region. He observed the Arab diners' conscientious eating habits and the Persian manner in which they meticulously held their napkins. Jerry opened his menu to peruse its exotic entrée selections, and also glanced alongside them for costs.

"Ted," Wolman whispered out of the side of his mouth, "there are no prices on my menu."

"The only menu with prices is being held by the gentleman seated at the end of the table," Dailey quietly educated his friend.

Wolman leaned forward and peeked down the length of the table and saw his host, a Middle Eastern man with a trimmed goatee, surrounded by an entourage. Propped back in his seat, Jerry wondered whether he was in the presence of royalty. They were never introduced.

Five pound lobsters, docile but very much alive, were brought forth by waiters to confront a large vat of steaming, boiling water. Wolman's eyes widened as white-gloved servers then forcefully submerged the crustaceans into the froth of the steel containers cooking them to reddened rigor-mortis. Jerry glanced at Ted, his only known ally at the table, and exhaled with particles of perspiration on his upper lip. Thereafter, everyone in attendance was gleeful, dipping lobster claws and tails in tureens of butter. Wolman felt as welcome as a guest at Old Original Bookbinder's. All went down well.

\*\*\*\*\*

When he returned to Washington, Wolman was able to keep bothersome bankers and cranky creditors at bay by assuring them that a deal was in the works and forthcoming. They took his assurances at his word and temporarily ceased their harassment. Life was now not without concerns, but reasonably bearable for Wolman. He could see flickering lights at the end of a traumatic tunnel. It had been nearly a year since headlines had brandished threatening doom at the wondrous Hancock Center. He had begged and borrowed through four full seasons to endure each passing day through to the next, so that the media and the rest of the world would not become cognizant of his struggles. But now, order was surely to be restored to his kingdom. The famed Wolman grin had suddenly regained its luminescence, accompanied by a renewed scrupulous swagger to his upper body.

Jerry made one more trip back to Paris that August. At the end of the last night's meeting, the representatives of the Kuwaiti investment group stood up as one to give a lengthy toast to Jerry. Embarrassed, Wolman quickly stood and orally followed suit. In a semi-circle, thousands of miles from Wolman's worldly possessions, all the men stood in accord.

Days later in Philadelphia, Jerry was eagerly urged by Ted Dailey to collect and send immediately all of the signed papers designating the transfer of his partners' shares over to Wolman. The papers were being signed with ease by one after another, until Jerry presented the documentation to Ed Snider, seated in the conference room of the Eagles office. Jerry approached the man he'd appointed Eagles Vice President and placed before him the authorization that would transfer Ed's interests over to Jerry in exchange for the promised $1,000,000. Ed tilted his head away, tightened his lips and refused to make eye contact with his boss.

"I'm not signing it," Snider remarked quietly.

"What do you mean?" Jerry queried, almost losing his balance in astonishment.

Ed shook his head tensely and negatively. Wolman heard Snider's crushing words that he would continue to play over and over again in his mind for decades. "I want to keep the hockey club," Snider decreed, and then looked up at his mentor for the first time.

"But Eddie, you already agreed," tried Wolman whose mouth had dried, mired in disbelief.

Snider got up to exit the uncomfortably awkward situation.

"Eddie, do you know what you're doing? It's not just the hockey club. I could lose *everything*. I'd be ruined!" pleaded Jerry, gesturing that his partner not leave the room.

"I'm not the only one that feels this way," Snider said coldly.

Wolman looked squarely into the eyes of the young man who had been the recipient and beneficiary of so much of his incalculable, habitual generosity.

"Eddie," Jerry's voice cascaded out of cadence in a last ditch effort, "if this is about money, we can work something out…"

"I'm not signing it," Ed growled in protest. Then he adjusted his glasses and left the room. Wolman watched as Snider exited the Eagles offices. Outside, the Eagles Vice President got into the back of Wolman's private limousine and was driven off.

Jerry raced to the phone and called Earl Foreman, frantically telling him what had just transpired. However, Wolman was just as surprised by his attorney's response. The reserved tone in Earl's voice was not terribly consoling, and his words next uttered spoke volumes.

"Jerry," Earl defended after a pause, "he's my brother-in-law."

From that moment on, the wedge of disloyalty had irreparably divided the three young Washingtonians who had ventured to Philadelphia together to conquer the city's sport's world. Foreman: the attorney; Snider: the administrator; and Wolman: the builder, the innovator and the money. They were never again to be a team.

# New Life

Disparaged, shocked and saddened, Wolman contacted Ted Dailey to inform him that Ed Snider had changed his mind regarding his interests and would not sign. In handling ninety-nine percent of Wolman's financing over his career, Dailey never once raised his voice. Upon hearing this news, Ted hollered at the top of his larynx directly into Wolman's ear. Malik and Seiler were together with Dailey in Paris. The men were furious to learn that the deal, along with their lucrative commissions, had been scarred and stifled. Jerry pleaded with Dailey to attempt to somehow steer and restructure the deal to the international group without the hockey club. A desperate Wolman encouraged him to do whatever it took by any means necessary to alter the proposed package and push it through. "Come on Ted, we've been in worse situations than this," Wolman tinkered with the truth.

Jerry likewise had to creatively consider re-maneuvering his assets around Snider's roadblock.

He knew that well over two hundred days had been booked at the Spectrum for NBA and NHL games, as well as miscellaneous special events in the upcoming year. He saw the soon-to-be-built arena as a solid cash cow with viable tenants to amply service his debts. The Spectrum had anticipated gross revenue in excess of $4,000,000 in the first year, a powerful asset toward Wolman's negotiations. On the other hand, he didn't believe that the infant hockey enterprise would be profitable for the first several years. He was willing to wager that he and Dailey could convince the Arab clique that the Spectrum outweighed the hockey enterprise by far. No doubt, because of Snider's demand, the hockey team had to be taken out of the mix. Wolman was left with little choice but to preserve the remainder of his concluded, but now clogged refinancing endeavor. Jerry felt it essential to acquire full ownership of the 15,000 foot arena, clearing Snider out of the way of the Spectrum's stock that Ed had been given as a plumb by the builder months prior. Therefore, Wolman had Earl Foreman intercede and negotiate a full transfer of Wolman's shares in the Flyers to Snider in exchange for Snider's stock in the Spectrum arena.

On August 26th, 1967, the swap occurred. Jerry Schiff, who accommodated Wolman, also sold his shares to Snider. Consequently, Ed Snider now enjoyed majority control of the Philadelphia Flyers.

\*\*\*\*\*

Every single employee could feel the friction and tension at Eagles headquarters. To his credit, Wolman had built up the morale of the Eagles office personnel over his four-year tenure. That ambiance had been rendered moot. The Eagles owner no longer spoke with Snider, his obstinate Vice President, who was also confronting Coach Kuharich over a multitude of his personnel decisions on and off the field. Rumors were spreading a dark swath over business affairs, and upper management's internal strife was reaching a breaking point. The Eagles operations were tangled and trapped in uncertainty and into chaos.

Then, in September of 1967, as Wolman's decimated dynasty continued wobbling, he received a surprise Western Union wire drafted by the hand of Ted Dailey, whose persistence had remained a tour de force in Paris. Ted's painstaking efforts to restructure the deal overseas resulted in the telegram's laconic lingo:

"TRANSACTION COMPLETELY ACCEPTED STOP... HAVE BEEN ASSURED OF A SETTLEMENT IN FULL AMOUNT STOP...TOO MUCH FOR CABLE OR PHONE HOWEVER I ASSURE YOU THEY ARE ACCEPTABLE STOP"

Jerry's eyes welled. Visions of his wife and children whom he'd barely seen for six months had in that moment come to his mind. The haggard owner saw a blurred new life between his lids and lashes.

One challenging long month proceeded after initial final draft letters of intent had been signed. Documentation needed to be gathered for presentation of the plethora of papers at settlement surrounding Wolman's multifarious properties and holdings. The Kuwaiti investment group dissected every single piece as if it were written on papyrus. It demanded updated title policies along with the preparation of pristine appraisals on every single property. Wolman appeased the group, and without being able to afford others' assistance, worked twenty-two hour days, seven days a week.

At the same time, Wolman's phones continued to ring around the clock from creditors asking when they'd get paid. Never ducking, Jerry answered each one. It became an alarming amalgamation of callousness from many whom he least expected, men he'd done business with for over a decade; some whom he'd made rich. Wolman felt as if he owed money to half the world.

Later that month, Jerry invited Ayub Malik to an Eagles football game to personally witness and enjoy the success of a professional football franchise in America. After the game, Jerry drove the representative of the foreign princely interests, to show him firsthand many of the soon–to-be re-mortgaged properties.

On Friday, October 13th, 1967, Wolman traveled to Paris to personally deliver all of the thickly bound documentation, including signed partnership interests, appraisals and title policies.

At an apartment in Paris, Wolman again mingled famously with the Middle Eastern brokers. In the recesses of his mind, he agonized over the fact that it was the eve of the Jewish holiday Yom Kippur. He'd always fasted every year of his life from sundown the night before through to sundown the next day. Abstaining was religiously required on this highest Holy Day. Wolman ate plentifully, but painfully after the moon had arisen that evening, scarfing his food and washing it down with wine. Unable to risk insulting his Arabian hosts, "What a man would not do for money?" he thought to himself guiltily. However, it had appeared as though the good Lord had rewarded and granted him with a blessed second chance.

Wolman arrived in Philadelphia the next day famished. The Eagles had a game scheduled against the San Francisco 49ers the day after on Sunday. Late that Saturday night, Leo Carlin, the young Eagles ticket man entered the office to do last minute preparations for the team's upcoming game, and noticed a light on in the owner's office. He could hear the tunneled sounds of Wolman's voice from under the office's shut door mumbling vigorously on the telephone. Carlin tiptoed gracefully with hesitation through the hallway to his boss's office. He knocked and slowly turned the knob to open the door as Wolman hung up the receiver.

"We got the money!" Jerry exclaimed at his assistant ticket manager, as his vocal chords cracked into a weeping invocation of emotion. $45,000,000 had been wired into an escrow account at the National Bank of California.

*****

On game day, the Eagles were stung by a gut-wrenching one-point loss to the Niners, 28-27. It was to be a foreboding oracle of lingering prophecies. Soon thereafter, Wolman received an ominous phone call from Ted Dailey.

"Jerry, it's Ted," Dailey spoke with difficulty, choosing his words carefully, laden with pauses. Ted's tone was incredulous but somber. "The deal fell through."

Wolman listened silently as the Persian rug was pulled out from under him. The broker explained that when Malik and Seiler had finally submitted the new deal directly to the Prince in Dubai, His Highness reacted irately to the absence of the hockey team. Dailey relayed that the Prince had then screamed at his men, tore up the papers and demanded that everyone exit the room.

"I was there," Dailey said faintly as if the carbon particles in his telephone's speaker were afraid to move. Wolman absorbed the news of the misfortune in silence as his eyes involuntarily closed. He had once again been blindsided.

"We thought we honestly had it, Jerry," consoled Dailey. "I'm sorry." Nothing more was spoken.

Wolman hung up the phone a destroyed man. For the first time since the beginning of all of his struggles, he felt overpowering anger and rage. Throughout his entire career, he had never fired anybody that had ever worked for him. Doing so was simply not in his nature. But, after traveling overseas several times, spending months scraping together every cent he could to keep his refinancing hopes alive, he was injured by whom he believed had taken his deal down the drain. Wolman was seething at Ed Snider.

*****

At the Spectrum's Dedication Ceremonies the next day, celebrating its record-time completion, all of the cities' big-wigs shook hands and patted one another's backs under a canopy on the new arena's steps. The Philadelphia Flyers were to play their first game the following night, and a genuine feeling of accomplishment and excitement had filled the air. However, Jerry Wolman, the arena's champion was nowhere nearby, nor to be found. Instead, Anne Wolman presented Philadelphia's City Council President Paul D'Ortona with an honorary key to the building. Jerry was in no condition to appear. Mentally embarrassed and physically drained, he had begged his wife at home, who despised public speaking, to appear on his behalf and say a few words to the attending crowd. Though strongly out of her comfort zone, Anne courageously agreed, masking her discomfort. She carried the ceremonies forward with graciousness.

Meanwhile, at the same time the crowd was applauding her husband's splendid sports arena, a defeated Wolman drove south on the I-95 Beltway to Baltimore to the law offices of Tatlebaum and Tatlebaum, to discuss whatever options were available for declaring bankruptcy.

# The Firing

Jerry retained the counsel of two major law firms, in Philadelphia (Wexler Mulder & Wiseman) and in Baltimore (Tatlebaum & Tatlebaum). Wolman met with representatives from both firms that day in Maryland to discuss his lamentable legal options.

Both firms' suggestions centered upon the builder/owner's filing of a straight Chapter VII Bankruptcy Petition. He was told that this would entail the necessity of a Trustee's appointment by the Bankruptcy Court to manage his extensive holdings; and that all of the assets would then be sold. Any balances recovered from the sales would thereafter be divided to satisfy the secured creditors' claims. Jerry carefully read through the general information provided him, then looked at his group of attorneys inquisitively.

"What would happen to the unsecured creditors, mostly my subcontractors?" he asked.

After reviewing the case law with their client, the attorneys demonstrated that in the event he were to file in the manner of a straight Chapter VII, his "unsecured" creditors would potentially receive a paltry, or in some cases, no pecuniary return on the monies owed to them. Jerry continued his questioning and determined that filing in Chapter VII would not allow unsecured creditors to recoup more than ten cents on the dollar. He combed his right hand through his hair in exasperation and frustration. This was unacceptable to him given the number of unsecured creditors, roughly one-third of the $85,000,000 he owed.

The Tatlebaum firm brought to his attention another option.

He was advised that he could file a Chapter XI Petition under the Bankruptcy Code. That was aimed more specifically for the benefit of unsecured creditors, and permitted Wolman to act as a debtor in possession of his holdings. Jerry was counseled that under the jurisdiction of the courts and a Creditors' Committee, he could at least attempt to obtain the maximum amount for his assets. That way, his unsecured creditors could participate in the retrieval and disbursement of money. The attorneys discussed that Wolman would have the opportunity to propose to work out a plan of arrangement satisfactory to the court and the Creditors' Committee.

The lawyers attempted to settle Jerry down citing that the safe, prudent course was to file the Chapter VII Petition and more easily withstand the epic financial melee.

"You're still a very young man," one of the lawyers reminded him. All advised him to protect himself fully, wash away the debt and start over.

Leaving the offices, Jerry's ego was still persuading him to fight and win whatever battles were on the horizon outside of bankruptcy. But those notions were restrained by his ingrained need to see others make gains from his enterprises, not falter with losses from them. His self-worth had been predicated on helping others prosper. Now, with his finances collapsing around him, at least he could hope to salvage those who had worked for him.

While driving back on the I-95 beltway, he mulled over his choices, but his thoughts and feelings swerved toward the direction of his perceived betrayal that had caused his failed financing.

*****

The next day in the late afternoon at his Eagles office, Jerry's emotions boiled over. Before leaving, Ed Snider haughtily walked past his boss in the hallway without saying a word. It was the first time Jerry had seen his protégé since the former had received the deal-ending phone call from Ted Dailey. Wolman turned around furiously, projecting the angst and anguish of his lost fortune, and watched the young man in shined shoes and dark-rimmed glasses saunter out to head home for the day. Jerry had been livid for two noxious days since the financing deal had fallen through. He viewed Snider's instant snubbing in the hallway as a smarting, glib reminder of Ed's disloyalty. The deal and his own balance sheet's remnants were figuratively in the coffin. Wolman literally had nothing more to lose.

Snider took the Eagles' limo home. Jerry slowly ambled outside as if in a trance and hailed a cab. He watched the taxi's meter all the way to Ed's house in suburban Philadelphia. He entered the abode and marched uninterrupted up the steps to Snider's bathroom where the new Flyers majority owner was preparing for the big season-opening hockey premiere. Standing in his jockey shorts, with recently applied shaving cream on his face, Ed appeared startled by the agitated fiery expression of his Eagles' boss in the mirror.

"What are you doing here?" Snider turned around cautiously.

"Eddie," Wolman fumed, "I came to tell you to your face. I want you to know you're fired."

"You can't fire me," Snider recoiled. "I've got a contract."

"You're no longer with the Eagles," the owner shot back, "don't come to work tomorrow!" Disgusted, Wolman then left the house he had afforded his former employee.

*****

As expected, Jerry received a phone call from Earl Foreman within the hour, admonishing Wolman, alleging that he did not have the authority to dismiss his Vice President.

"The last time I checked," Wolman clamored, "I *still* own fifty-two percent of the team, and I can fire whoever I want!"

Snider and Foreman drove to New York the next day to meet with Commissioner Rozelle. The brothers-in-law presented a formal complaint in an attempt to reverse Snider's dismissal. The Commissioner was sympathetic, but unwilling to intervene, citing that the dispute over the firing was a personal team matter.

Within moments of the duo leaving Rozelle's office, the Commissioner telephoned his dear friend, Jerry. Rozelle wanted Wolman to know that he had fully supported his decision, but left the owner with a very specific cautionary warning to be careful with regard to the two men.

By the time Snider and Foreman had returned from the NFL league offices, a news media brouhaha was stirring over the front office firing. Every reporter in the city wanted to know why the important Eagles VP had unexpectedly been cut from the team. Rumors fluttered like bats in a cave that a rift between Snider and Kuharich had become far too intolerable. Publicly, Snider seemed incredulous at being the victim of an unfair removal. Wolman refused to make any comment, and after the three men had met privately, so did Foreman or Snider.

Out of genuine concern for Snider's wife and children, the owner inscribed on an Eagles memo pad: "Dear Eddie: I have told Joe King [Eagles business manager] to continue your pay for six months,…Jerry." Terms were later reached on a buy-out settlement of Ed's contract.

That Sunday, October 22nd, 1967, CBS cameramen zoomed in on the Eagles owner standing alone on the sidelines at the ten yard line of the Eagles game in St. Louis' Busch Stadium. His team was losing in lop-sided fashion to the Cardinals. The close-ups captured the stoic essence of the man, dark-eyed from solitary struggles, revealing his solemn, affectless countenance nationwide.

*****

Wolman continued traveling the next week in perpetual motion, hoping to acquire significant financing, albeit to no avail. He had flown into JFK airport in New York where he called his wife Anne after having returned from a last ditch trip to Switzerland. Her voice was replete with concern for him. They had received notification in that day's mail that their utility and electrical services would soon be turned off if payment did not occur immediately. Wolman leaned his head forward against the glass of the payphone's suffocating cubicle, embarrassed and trembling. He assured his wife, promising her that he would handle the matter as soon as he got home that evening.

Then, by habit, he dialed the Eagles office and learned that there was an urgent message from Earl Foreman. When Jerry called Earl,

Foreman told him that it was very important that he and Eddie meet with him in person immediately.

"Can't it wait?" Jerry asked, as he had just gone without sleep and had traveled for hours on end, hadn't eaten and needed to get home. Foreman was adamant that it was extremely imperative and paramount that Jerry meet them at the Locust Club in center city Philadelphia in two hours.

Driving from New York in a state of mental paralysis, Jerry was dazed by the self-concocted, delirious notion that perhaps his longtime friends had somehow experienced an epiphany. Wolman believed there was compassion in both men; compassion in all men.

Jerry stopped first for a much needed Snickers bar on the way to the members-only entrance of the Locust Club. Upon entering the social establishment and seeing how nicely the occupants were dressed, he was reminded that he hadn't shaved in four days. A staff member escorted him to a private room where Foreman, Snider and Lou Stein, President of the Food Fair supermarket chain, sat around a conference table. Wolman recalled Lou Stein as one of the men he had managed to outbid that fateful day in December of 1963 to acquire the Eagles. Jerry stood frozen with curiosity. He never sat down. Eddie and Earl never said a word. Before Wolman could ask why he had been directed there, the men presented Jerry with a contract to sign.

"What's this?" Wolman asked. "What's going on here?"

Jerry's vision, faulty from fatigue, tried to focus on the papers. The contents had been drawn, as he pieced together the wording, for the purpose of his selling the Philadelphia Eagles to the three men silently facing him.

"I'm not signing this," Jerry scoffed, "I'd never sell the Eagles." The magnitude of the force of the moment was hitting him all at once. Wolman looked at Earl Foreman, his former best friend and right arm in business. He recalled the look on his face the day he bought him a Cadillac ten years earlier. Branded on his mind was the moment the two clasped hands at the Bellevue Stratford Hotel on the day they learned they would have the Eagles.

He turned slightly to peer into the eyes of Ed Snider, and was reminded of the day that he picked up an unkempt Ed on a street corner in Washington, and had offered to help him. Now it was Jerry who was glum and unshaven, though no one was coming to his aid. Wolman had furnished the two men with unimaginable offerings of prosperity throughout their business and personal lives.

This most unimaginable scrivener's demand had been handed to him in a time of personal destitution.

"If you don't sign this," threatened Stein menacingly, "we're gonna make trouble for you!"

Everything that had fallen numb inside Wolman became quivering to life.

"Let me tell you something," Jerry stiffened his back and his vocal chords at the men. "I've got to get home because they're turning my lights off, my water off, and repossessing my cars. And you think you're gonna make *trouble for me?*"

Wolman threw the dastardly paperwork back on the conference table and drove home on fumes and fuming, to his wife and family in Chevy Chase, Maryland.

# The Press Conference

Jerry opened the door to his home late that night and ran through his house to embrace the warmth of his family. He had lost all faith in people's decency for the moment, but his wife and children quickly provided him with their expected unconditional love and support.

Wolman then raced to take a much needed shower and shave, but was unable to cleanse himself of his worries. Sifting late at night through a stack of more than half a week's mostly threatening mail, he came across a letter from Ted Dailey. He tore the envelope open before surveying all others. Handwritten on Pan Am stationery while flying over the Atlantic Ocean, his broker had expressed the simple empathy and care that an injured Wolman had prematurely sought that day:

*Dear Jerry,*

*As I write this I am on the flight home. Obviously I have taken this whole thing very seriously and I am sure you are aware I take its ending the same way. Please don't let this get to you. The strength, ability, and fortitude that you have shown during this last year only proves what a terrific guy you are. Many people have had the same problems you are now having, but few have come back. I have been so close to you during this past year that I know you can work your way back. Please don't stop trying. My heart goes out to you, Anne and the kids. I am now and I will always be*

*Your Friend,*

*Ted*

He carefully folded the letter, placed it back in its envelope and into his robe's right pocket. With a renewed energy and hope in the notion of "friendship" partially restored, Jerry went to sleep that night next to Anne, and awoke refreshed with a goal to set for his most important priority in business. One way or another, he had to find a method to hold on to the Philadelphia Eagles.

But bad luck persisted as his only form of luck, and multiplied. On November 3rd, Jerry received word from his attorney Hy Tatlebaum that American Seating Company, the group that had installed 15,000 seats in the Spectrum, had filed a lien against him. Wolman still owed the company $174,000 as the balance due on the $600,000 job. However, of all his extensive financial obligations, the debt to the seating corporation was relatively under control in comparison. Best efforts had been and were being made to continue to close the indebtedness gap. The lien came unexpectedly.

Tatlebaum advised Jerry to move quickly to file a Chapter VII as many creditors would now aggressively dash to be at the front of the collection line. The lawyer was right. Subsequently, nearly a dozen creditors followed suit, suing Wolman for substantial amounts he didn't have. The self-made multi-millionaire was facing a downward off-ramp toward a bankruptcy exit. Against the advice of his legal counsel, however, his genuine concern for his partners and creditors got the best of him. Wolman made the decision to choose a Chapter XI Arrangement and dedicate his time and efforts to make everything right and everyone whole.

\*\*\*\*\*

The press began treating Wolman's unraveling fate as a front page gossip tabloid. For the first time, the football owner's financial problems were engraved on newspapers' pages for all to unfold and see. The newly targeted infamous owner couldn't make a move without discrediting stories appearing in print, on the radio or on television. And if that weren't corrosive enough, he had to deal with unnecessary delirium, because the stories were unfounded and/ or untrue. Headlines such as: "WOLMAN SELLS EAGLES TO LOMBARDI!" rocked the city like an earthquake. Rogue rumors began to blather that Jerry's money streams were being floated by "gangster money." Jerry had little time to separate truths from fodder. Therefore, at 8:30 a.m. on November 14th, 1967, Wolman gave a press conference to clean the air over his troubling misfortune.

Jerry sat behind a table on which rested a microphone, to delineate his difficulties to the citizenry. He took a long drag of his lit cigarette and revealed that he was indeed confronted with a severe shortage of cash and limited time. Denying the claim of current insolvency, he emphasized that his listed assets of $92,000,000 out-valued his liabilities of $85,000,000. Admittedly, however, Wolman needed an infusion of at least $7,000,000 in cash to remain solvent. He went on the record that he was completely at the mercy of his creditors to whom he was shackled by millions of monetary handcuffs.

Using the forum then to reach out to those he owed, Wolman publicly detailed a plan for repayment contingent and dependent on his creditors' sustained patience. He put forward a proposal that asked for time, six months to a year, to sell off his properties. He calculated repaying claims at a rate of twenty percent down and the balance within eighteen months: one hundred Lincoln cents on the dollar. Taking another drag from his diminishing Lucky Strike, he readily confessed that everything he owned was for sale, with the exception of his gridiron Eagles. Jerry almost gloated into the green-eyed news cameras' lenses, stating with surly conviction that his football team will never be purchasable. "I wouldn't sell the Philadelphia Eagles for $150,000,000."

The frail forty-year-old blew smoke and answered questions for two hours, but never lost his consummate sense of humor that had captivated the city over the last four years. "On my ride over here this morning," he recalled, "I listened to a radio news report on my finances." Wolman paused and glanced around the room. "Boy, was it disastrous."

Earlier that morning, Jerry's fingernails had in fact tightly gripped the seat of his car while he listened to the announced assessments that he had overdrawn his bank account by $85,000, owed $182,000 in back taxes, and was $226,000 overdue in paying his insurance premiums.

The press conference caught the attention of the national press, and *Time* magazine soon ran a feature detailing Wolman's dramatic plight. Over the next several days, onlookers across the country were buzzing with "did-you-see's" regarding the gaunt Wolman conundrum. But something seemed different with this particular prominent person's fall from grace. Many found it difficult not to sympathize with and pull for the still-smiling Cinderella transplant from Shenandoah, Pennsylvania, who had started with less than glass slippers.

The purpose of the press conference had been to bare his chest and offer a palpable plan to ebb the tide of incoming lawsuits which might force him into a bankruptcy boat without a paddle. Despite a comprehensive, coherent performance on that morning, Wolman soon realized that most creditors would not be patient through a riptide.

# Chapter XI

Following his press conference, Wolman decided to meet his creditors face to face hoping to fortify his message and foster their allegiance. Several hundred of them, ninety percent of whom were his subcontractors, packed a conference room at the Marriot Hotel just over Philadelphia's city line, to hear out the details of his plan in person.

Jerry looked around the Marriott's carpeted Conference Center room at the seated men who had worked with and for him more than a dozen successive and successful years. He knew the names associated with every face. With many, he could picture their wives and children as well.

Wolman had done business with a multitude of the men without a written contract, nothing simpler than the trusting thrust of shaken hands. To most he had been their champion; to others he was just "Jerry." However, each individual present in the hotel's hall shared one common denominator: Jerry Wolman owed him money.

After standing up unflinchingly to address his listeners, he described his proposals outlining his intentions and methods from behind a podium for almost an hour. At the conclusion of his speech, the once invincible industrialist spoke in a cadence from the beat of his heart.

"For years, I've completed many jobs that I couldn't have done without you," Jerry asserted. "My work now is *for* you," he continued. "I'm here today to make certain that each of you gets every dime that I owe you."

Wolman's creditors, unaccustomed to hearing such sincere frankness from an owner, rose to their feet and provided him with rip-roaring and rousing applause which resounded well into the hotel lobby. A line formed approaching the front forum and men offered new handshakes toward unity of purpose. Jerry wrapped both his arms around the shoulders of general contractors and subs closing in on both sides of him.

In order for his proposed plans to work, however, he needed unified acceptance by everyone. The following afternoon, three of his less familiar creditors unkindly sued, setting off an avalanche of nearly twenty-five liens that fell like jagged boulders for ten straight days. A band of banking institutions, including Wolman's local Old Line National Bank of Rockville, jumped into the fray with wringing legal pressures. "Time" was what Wolman had needed. But the clock's hands were ticking perilously close to midnight on his Cinderella story.

On the afternoon of Wednesday, December 13th, 1967, stamped as case #13072, Jerry Wolman, the former hitch-hiking paint store manager turned renowned building tycoon and professional sports owner, filed in Chapter XI for an Arrangement under the protection of the Bankruptcy Act. Against the advice of his attorneys to file under Chapter VII in order to more easily discard his debts, Wolman opted to better protect and benefit his unsecured creditors.

Shuddering from the premonition that newspapers would run the event as a monumentally maligning story, Jerry couldn't bring himself to go with his attorneys to the clerk of bankruptcy court for filing. Instead, he fled home to speak to his family before the press' anticipated headlines. Subdued and hemorrhaging with guilt, this day of reckoning supplied the darkest doldrums of his recent blackest months.

Anne and their two children, Helene now seventeen and Alan just fifteen, listened without interruption to their father in his den. He deftly explained the financial and legal ramifications of his situation, concluding by stressing how important his family was to him. Emotions ran high.

Before dinner that evening, Jerry went to his bedroom and noticed an envelope pinned to his pillow with handwritten cursive in blue ink that spelled "Dad." Inside, Jerry discovered a short note along with two $18,000 checks made out to his order from each child. The sum equaled the amounts he had placed in their respective savings accounts during the previous year.

The note read, *"Dear Dad: We hope this helps.*

*Love,*

*Helene and Alan. "*


Jerry immediately called his children into his bedroom and told them he could not accept their gesture.

"I can't take this money, this is yours," he told them softly.

His daughter Helene placed her hand on her father's. "Dad, this is *our* money."

Wolman saw in the gaze of his offspring how much their contributing meant to them. He embraced both children at the same time and capitulated, against his grain, to accept their maturity and their gift.

In the evening after dinner, Jerry and his family drove to the Hot Shoppe for fudge sundaes. The family kept up an admirable sense of humor, lightly joshing with each other about the events of the day over tasty desserts. Nevertheless, that night Wolman attempted to rest in bed, eyes open to the blank void of light, ears noting nothing, as cramps circled his stomach in tactile knots.

"Life is strange," he thought to himself with his head fitted in the crease of the pillow.

When he used to walk into a room at a social gathering, the band would routinely begin to play the climactic chords of the tune "Hail to the Chief." After his financial scrapes had been aired to the world over the past year, his invitations to dozens of social events per month had been eviscerated. They had come to an end. Friends seemed fewer and farther.

# The Fund Drive

Christmas approached at the speed of twinkling decorative light. For Jerry, it was impossible to replicate the hundreds of gifts that he had sent each year to so many employees and business friends. Court orders and sagging, depleted bank accounts had frozen Wolman's best intentions and customs. Nor could he provide annual bonuses, given the strict restrictions placed upon him by his bankruptcy. Jerry pensively paced in a nearly penniless pattern through his hallways, agonizing over his inability to continue his personal and company traditions. He discovered that these legal barriers did not apply to those corporations or companies not directly involved within the court's jurisdiction; such as the Philadelphia Eagles. Therefore, he was able to reward his faithful Eagles' employees with thoughtful gifts and well-deserved bonuses from the flow of the franchise's gains. He found a way to briefly feel again like life was worth living by giving. He was more gratified than at any other time in the last tumultuous year.

The Wolman family went into semi-hibernation at the end of 1967, foregoing holiday celebrations out of consternation and necessity. Jerry's feelings of isolation and loneliness continued to persist as he braced himself for his upcoming bankruptcy court proceedings. He redoubled his efforts and concentration in the New Year on not letting his partners or creditors get hurt. But, every step he took was foreshadowed. It seemed no one was on his side.

While very few of his well-off friends and high-society associates came to Wolman's aid, unbeknownst to Jerry, offers to help the bankrupt former millionaire began to sprout from one amazingly unexpected place.

*****

It was the gloomiest, most dank day in Shenandoah when Wolman had filed for bankruptcy. The town's favorite son embodied the glory and glamour of an authentic hero. Through rags and riches, Jerry had never once turned his back on his hard, shiny-coal heritage. Besides making countless philanthropic contributions, he habitually returned to his Pennsylvania home year after year, and sat, drank and ate comfortably in the hospitality of its men and women.

A few weeks after Wolman's court filing, something uncontrollable started to snowball among the good people of Shenandoah. In a folkloric fourth dimension, and with a human's seventh sense, Willie Robel launched and coordinated a dramatic drive to raise funds to help her husband's best friend, Jerry.

It all began when the Eagles equipment manager's wife placed an ad in the Personals section of the hometown newspaper. The notice simply began: *"Jerry Wolman has always helped everybody all his life. Now he needs our help, so let's help him."*

She included an address for those to send money, hoping to augment support for her fabled friend, and to raise his spirits and outlook. The published request noted that a complete record of the contributions would be kept, and that over time the offerings would be repaid to the donors.

Word circulated about the fund drive with a sonic boom throughout the mining town, and the results were nothing short of astounding. Legions of people in the entire region dropped everything but their humble, helpful natures in order to contribute. Astonishingly, in a matter of days, Willie had received over $1,000,000 from the hardnosed, classy workers and their families. Her efforts cascaded over into a country-wide wishing well of well-wishers. Willie's firm objective was to raise $7,000,000 to rescue Jerry from trouble. She gauged that at the rate donations were flooding in, she would raise $5,000,000 by the end of the following week.

However, a phone call from Jerry, who had just been made

aware of what had transpired, proscribed her from achieving her miraculous goal.

"I'll never forget what you're trying to do for me, Willie," Wolman told her with deep sentiment, "but I can't accept it." Times were certainly most difficult, but Jerry persuaded her that he could never live with himself if he ever took money from those less advantaged, but decadently decent people. She pleaded with him to reconsider, but his refusal was final.

The following day on January 12th, 1968, the *Philadelphia Daily News* ran the story and interviewed Mrs. Robel:

"I was really not surprised," she said, "I've been saying all along that he [Wolman] is a giver, not a taker. He'll never change, but I'm sorry it didn't turn out the way we were hoping."

\*\*\*\*\*

That same day, the *Daily News* included a letter that had been sent to the Eagles offices by a twelve-year-old newspaper boy in the twilight of his childhood. It read:

*"My name is James and I am 12 years old. Me and my brother Johnny play for the little Eagles. Our neighborhood team didn't do too good this year, ending in third or fourth place. But that isn't no disgrace, not like them banks and people who don't want to help you Mr. Wolman. Most of the players are paperboys and we're proud to wear the colors of the big Eagles. We had a meeting and we want to help you.*

*Maybe you don't remember, but you did a lot of good things. You let us play at your field two years ago after the big game was over. You gave us hot chocolate and blankets to keep us warm.*

*Now we want to help you. Tell us what to do."*

# Bankruptcy Court

The previous 1966 season, the Philadelphia Eagles had played fiercely and skillfully enough to earn consideration among the elite playoff contending football teams in the NFL. However, as the uncertainties surrounding its owner manifested into the hesitation of the team's players and coaches, the Eagles retreated to a 6-7-1 record during the 1967 campaign. As the season lunged forward, each negative rumor and every corresponding press release stymied and stalled the struggling team. Personnel focus and identity lolled backward into field-lethargy. Distracted and consumed, Wolman's own epicenter of battles would play out between the hash marks of the biggest bankruptcy case ever filed in the state of Maryland.

A month following the '67 Eagles final game, The Washington Post ran a front page article on January 19th, 1968 that shed new light on the severity of Wolman's circumstances. At his first creditors' meeting in court, an emotion-choked Jerry had revealed that his total cash on hand was $24.09, accompanied by a $35 savings bond. The appointed Referee, (soon-to-be-Judge) Joseph Kaiser, gave the debtor Wolman, who held encumbered assets valued in the tens of millions, ninety days to come with a plan to get out of his predicament.

Eager to begin to disentangle matters and move on, Wolman spent his first two months in bankruptcy working alongside his attorneys, trying to figure out the best plan of arrangement to satisfy the courts, his secured and unsecured creditors. Jerry soon learned he had to answer to a new patriarch: the Creditors' Committee.

Formed to oversee the various plans of arrangement set forth by Wolman, the members seemed dreadfully unhurried and unwilling to pursue Jerry's aggressive actions. His first proposed plan entailed raising funds by favorably negotiating sales to reputable outside private investors. But a happy medium as to terms or pricing could never be reached among the Creditors' Committee and the investors. Wolman's initial attempt was never accepted, and fizzled.

As time moved on, Wolman grew wearily cognizant of three crucial dependent variables. First, after having listed and submitted the names of approximately three hundred creditors to the Referee, Wolman was indomitably determined to get each and every person compensated.

Second, Jerry had twenty-five partners and friends whom he had brought into the building business. He had personally arranged for the complete financing of twelve substantial apartment building properties that glaringly remained in his dissolving and declining empire. These partners had enjoyed the high life with Jerry in the best times, but now all of their futures were frightfully linked to Wolman's demise.

Third, Wolman was unwavering in his diehard conviction to retain his ownership of the Philadelphia Eagles. His attorneys had Jerry believing that an appropriate plan of arrangement could take as little as the ninety days the judge had been seeking in which to satisfy all parties involved. The lawyers had grossly miscalculated.

*****

Filing for bankruptcy had temporarily relieved some of the pressure that he had been experiencing because lawsuits were stopped in their tracks. However, that was just the calm before the storm. Wolman soon faced an onslaught of those secured creditors asking Judge Kaiser for the rights to file immediate foreclosures against the debtor's assets.

Kaiser took the position that there might be sufficient funds in the secured assets that could carry over to unsecured creditors. The court therefore denied the requests to foreclose. Wolman was relieved to be working with a referee who shared his intentions of getting all participants as close to a full return of money as possible. But the judge would not rule out of hand in favor of Jerry's requests to take the Eagles out of all equations for relief.

Precisely when all of Wolman's troubles could not be exceeded, Mother Nature wickedly interceded. On March 1st, 1968, a severe South Philly windstorm caused a section of the roof of the Spectrum arena to lift off during a live performance of the Ice Capades. This costly and embarrassing headache reminded Wolman of his debacle in Chicago. Lightning had struck Jerry twice, now with high winds to make the welts more worrisome. The public relations and political nightmares were made horrifying due to public safety concerns. (The perforated Spectrum arena, through its controlling entity Spectrum Arena, Inc., would inevitably be swept into a separate involuntary reorganization under Chapter X in Pennsylvania's Eastern District on May 1st, 1968.)

With pressure mounting, Wolman provided a plan of arrangement on April 22nd, 1968 that would create a new company, Jerry Wolman Enterprises, Inc. to be sold publicly. The plan anticipated raising $36,750,000, of which a net of $12,000,000 would be loaned to Wolman to pay off the secured creditors. Jerry's majority ownership of the Eagles would be the security for the loan. "Enterprises" assets were to include 100% of The Spectrum Arena, Inc. (soon to be forced into bankruptcy), Connie Mack Stadium Limited Partnership and the Yellow Cab Companies. The Eagles could not be included because the NFL forbade public ownership. The plan was finally approved by the Committee.

However, when the Securities and Exchange Commission dragged its heels delaying the sale of the stock to the public, and after the Spectrum's cover had been blown, secured creditors applied to Judge Kaiser to force the sale of the Eagles to satisfy Jerry's debts. Day by day, the court became more and more adamant that it was time to liquidate everything: including The Philadelphia Eagles.

Frustrated by the dawdling Creditors' Committee, the SEC, the Spectrum's reorganization and the judge's dogged intent upon imminent liquidation, the eternal optimist inside Jerry was becoming painfully aware that his reality was between bedrock and the hardest place. Through his proffered plans, he had attempted creatively to shake the money-trees of outside investors and public stock offerings, to no avail. Jerry had lost his grip on the branches he thought could blossom. They had been sawed off at the trunk.

*****

Jerry, for the moment, centered his catastrophe-avoidance thoughts upon his many apartment and office complexes and his more than two dozen partners. They had negative capital accounts due to depreciation; they also had an obligation to file claims in the bankruptcy proceedings for the benefit of the partnerships. Once having done so, the partners would have the same benefits as other unsecured creditors. However, if the properties themselves were foreclosed by judicial fiat, Jerry's associates would lose any equity in the buildings and would risk being liable for any deficits that would occur on account of the first mortgage. Recognizing that his own troubles were now irreparable, Jerry sat up late into the night mulling over his inescapability. Moreover, he contemplated that he wasn't alone in the misfortunes he had built.

That night he had a brainstorm worth brandishing. Wolman conceived of a proposal to clean the calamitous slate of his apartment and office building properties and, at the same time, provide a legal safe haven for salvaging his partners' finances. In an unusual turn of events, Jerry, with the approval of the court, traded all of his ownership interests in his apartment and office buildings to his partners in exchange for their waiving claims against him in the proceedings. When those claims had been waived, the other unsecured creditors would be able to receive a larger percentage of the millions of dollars newly available toward their own claims. All gained, and saved Jerry's partners from forced firehouse sales and huge losses. Only Wolman walked away with nothing from a formerly celebrated, booming apartment and office building legacy he had built, shared with others and had then given away. The partners went on to make fortunes within a few years' time after the markets had recovered.

# The Understated Heroine

At least three days a week, Jerry appeared at court in Baltimore, futilely attempting to negotiate with the Creditors' Committee or fend off lawsuits asking for leave to foreclose; oftentimes without enough money for gas to drive to the courtroom.

After one particularly long day of legal torments, he slumped into his home to the sympathetic sight of his wife in the foyer. Anne Wolman greeted her husband with some cash collected between her fingers and palm, handing all of it to him. That day she had driven to town and had sold some of her personal jewelry. The previous week, she had vended a few valuable paintings and lithographs from their home. Over the months, she had sold practically everything she had, without a word, quietly rallying to her husband in need. Jerry had never known, nor would know, anyone like her. Unaffected and steady through Jerry's slide, Anne genuinely couldn't have cared less about losing everything. She never once cried nor made any bones about their unsavory situation.

"Don't worry," she told him rubbing the back of his neck, "we'll get through this."

But the constant pressure and stress were taking their toll on her stoic sentiments.

In late November of 1968, Jerry was seated, tilted back in his office looking over the travel itinerary for the upcoming Eagles nationally televised Thanksgiving Day football game, an NFL tradition. After a seamy stretch of eleven losses through the first eleven games of the season, the 1968 Eagles were unbearable to watch, the worst performing football team in the league. "Joe Must Go" chants and banners were unfurled in fury from 360 degrees at every home game. The athletes' play had been uninspiring and pitiful. The organization had attained disarray.

The Eagles, unfortunately, would be at center ring without a net in Detroit that week to play the Lions on Turkey Day. A respectable showing before the NFL's anticipated huge holiday audience meant a great deal to Wolman. His franchise was in dire need of infusions of dignity and respect.

That morning Jerry received a grave and harrowing phone call at his Eagles office. He was told that Anne had just been taken by ambulance to the Doctor's Hospital in Washington, D.C. Wolman quickly learned that she had been the victim of a heart attack at a mere thirty-eight years.

Jerry raced two hundred miles to her bedside, arriving with little memory of how he had reached his destination. Her skin was pale and blotchy, with lavender half-circles under her eyes. Tubes and medical devices and cords were intertwined all around her. Anne squeezed her shaken husband's hand and faintly whispered, "How are the kids?"

Dr. Paul Lichtman intervened, taking Jerry a few steps aside. The doctor and longtime mentor reviewed with Jerry his wife's genetic faulty valve condition that had caused a damaging heart attack. All of Wolman's problems disintegrated into one fearfully overwhelming concern for the love of his life.

*****

Anne Wolman was in all respects the soft-spoken angel of the Philadelphia Eagles; an extremely kind and active participant within the club's confines, adding her steady charisma during the five seasons that her husband had owned the team. She watched over practices, headed charitable events and had garnered exceedingly close connections with many of the players' wives. Everyone she touched looked up to her.

In Jerry Wolman's tenure, he had missed only one Eagles football game: to be with his wife on Thanksgiving in that Washington hospital room.

On November 28th, 1968, Eagles players gathered unsteadily in Detroit's visitor's locker room, visibly concentrating on the Wolmans in D.C. Minutes before walking out onto the playing field, Eagles captains rose from their stools. They were of one mind, and gestured to quiet the room. Each team leader repeated to the winless team a one-game challenge to play this special game to honor the ailing Anne Wolman. The burly oversized men dedicated their actions in unison to a crescendo of supportive conviction.

The 0-11 Philadelphia Eagles club won its first football game of the season that day, shutting out the Detroit Lions 12-0 in the rain before a nation of holiday viewers. Never once over four quarters did the emotionally-charged swarming Eagles defense allow the Lions to roar. Jerry and Anne had received word of the team's dedication before the game, and had watched the team's gritty effort on a small black and white hospital television set while holding each other's hands, fingers intertwined.

The next day, Eagles Defensive Tackle Floyd Peters traveled to D.C. with a few teammates. They presented Mrs. Wolman with the game ball signed by the entire team.

# LEONARd TOSE

By the fall of 1968, the judge had made it abundantly clear that he believed there was considerable equity in the Philadelphia Eagles to enhance the sums available for the unsecured creditors. He decreed that unless Wolman came up with an immediate plan of arrangement that encompassed the needs of those creditors, the football team should be added to the equation and sold.

Along with the judge, Jerry grew more and more frustrated and impatient throughout the year with the SEC, awaiting clearance for his public stock offering. The court would not wait any longer. With his objective to bring in the most capital for creditors, Kaiser decided that the Eagles should be promptly sold to the highest bidder at auction.

In order to sell the team, Jerry needed to have one hundred percent ownership and control of the team's corporate stock. He met uncomfortably with his former attorney, current Eagles partner Earl Foreman, face to face. On October 26th, 1968, with no viable choice available, Wolman agreed to pay Foreman and Ed Snider $2,600,000 from said sale for their interests in the football franchise. Under the terms, that money could be divided among the two men however they chose. All other ownership parties and factions agreed to amenable payment for their respective shares which had been given to them by Wolman.

A scheduled hearing was placed on the docket toward the end of the year for the purpose of airing preliminary bids to purchase the club. On that day, Kaiser raised the question, "Is anyone present interested in bidding on the team?"

Jerry heard a familiar voice emanating from the back of the courtroom. Earl Foreman stood up to announce that he would seriously consider making a bid. Foreman clarified his position, however, by pointing and alleging to the judge that Jerry Wolman's interest in the Philadelphia Eagles had little or no value since the asset had deteriorated considerably under his "mismanagement."

Shamelessly shocked by his former best friend's and counsel's appearance and words, Jerry's blood boiled over. "That's ridiculous," he stood up to shout. Kaiser then turned and directly posed his question to Wolman. "How much do *you* feel the team is worth?"

"Your Honor," Jerry blasted and boasted, "I believe the Eagles are worth," pausing for three seconds, "$16,000,000!" The courtroom's listeners emitted a united gasp, no one ever having heard of a professional team valued in that exalted range.

"Mr. Wolman," replied the judge, "you have ninety days to find someone who will pay that amount. If not, the team will be auctioned off to the highest bidder." Court was dismissed.

Jerry left the hearing with a defined mission based on his own pronouncement. And it was imperative that in the event he had to lose the Philadelphia Eagles, Hell would freeze over before he allowed the team to be bought by his adversaries at a bargain basement price founded falsely on bald aspersions against him.

*****

Debonair Leonard H. Tose, a well-healed, slim, fifty-year-old Norristown, Pennsylvania trucking operator, had been part of a group which had unsuccessfully underbid on the Eagles when Jerry was awarded the team in 1963. It was generally known that Tose had previously owned 1% of the Eagles in the late 1940's, and was at that time one of the sixty-five prominent local shareholders in the franchise prior to Wolman's ownership. A lifelong football devotee, Tose had briefly played collegiate football on the freshman team at the University of Notre Dame. And his veins had always flowed green at the mention of the Philadelphia Eagles. Never having met the affluent industrialist, Jerry returned to his office and, through a friend, set up an immediate, confidential meeting with Tose.

Tose arrived at the Eagles offices impeccably dressed in sharkskin-suited attire, accompanied by a curvaceous woman on his left arm and two bottles of Johnny Walker Red scotch under his right arm. After having asked his lovely female companion to wait outside Jerry's office, the two men sat therein to discuss the future of the football team. Tose plopped the bottles of liquor down on the desk as Jerry scoured for two glasses. Tose filled each with dense mahogany scotch. By the time Jerry had taken two toasty sips, Tose had conspicuously emptied his first glass, and had poured himself another. Jerry waived off any topping of his glass, wanting to sustain sobriety under the circumstances.

Over the course of their discussion, Wolman sensed how keenly his invited company coveted the football team. Their conversation continued into Leonard Tose's opening of the second bottle. Jerry had persuaded his guest that $16,000,000 for the organization was the best buy he'd ever make in his lifetime.

"The sport is gaining immense popularity, the league is expanding throughout the country and television contracts will continue to boom," Wolman contended to his engrossed potential buyer, "Why, within twenty years, the team will be worth $800,000,000!" That comment drew a facial glimmer from Tose. He had already been convinced.

Over the next weeks, attorneys representing each, negotiated and drafted a preliminary agreement. Under the terms thereafter approved by the bankruptcy court, if Wolman could not extricate himself from his debts by May 1st, 1969, and if Tose's bid remained the highest, then the latter would succeed the former as owner. The parties also agreed that Wolman had the right to repurchase the team if his plan of arrangement was successful.

*****

Anne Wolman remained in the hospital recovering. Jerry and the Eagles were finishing their most dismal season in franchise history. On December 15th, 1968, the Eagles played their last game of the year, hosting the Minnesota Vikings. On a brutally cold, snow-flurried day, the melancholic fans turned malevolent while watching a ridiculously concocted halftime presentation gone afoul. Frustrated by the franchise's spiraling decline, many of the fed-up onlookers began to boo with breaths visibly enhanced by alcohol. They threw snowballs aimed at "Santa Claus" struggling to entertain at mid-field. Fanatics pelted the pretend jolly Old Saint Nick with relentless cannonballs of hard-packed snow. "Philly Faithfuls" had already revealed a renowned cantankerous reputation for displaying displeasure, but this particular "baptism by snow" of a saint brought televised national attention. The incident would endure in unsavory folklore for generations.

The Eagles lost to the Vikings by the score of 24-17. Throughout the season, players and coaches had been perturbed by what was transpiring around the owner for whom they so dearly cared.

After the game, Wolman sat solemnly behind his desk with a bloated, bleak bulge in his gut. Barring a miracle, he would never attend another Eagles game as owner. The team's best player, All-Pro tackle Bob Brown tapped on Wolman's door, delicately sensing it was a bad time. There was otherwise no need to knock on a door that was forever open.

"Can I talk to you for a second?" the sweating lineman asked gently.

"Sure Bob," Wolman almost moaned as he gathered himself, "what can I do for you?"

"Jerry, I was thinking," the player began, "if it'll help you out in any way, you don't have to pay me my signing bonus." Under the terms of the tackle's contract, the Eagles still owed Brown $40,000 of his deferred signing bonus.

The owner rose from his seat. "That means a lot to me, Bob, thank you," he said shaking his head, "but it won't do me any good."

Jerry and Bob locked in a brief final embrace. When Wolman let go, the 1968 season and his ownership had truly ended.

# Sold

In the early morning of Thursday, May 1$^{st}$, 1969, in the conference
rooms on the 17$^{th}$ floor of the Packard Building at 15$^{th}$ and Chestnut
Streets, the two main principals Wolman and Tose, Wolman's
creditors, Eagles stockholders, attorneys and bankers went back
and forth attempting to close the complex sale of the Philadelphia
Eagles.

By 3:30 p.m. in the afternoon, dozens of reporters and radio-TV
technicians lingered restively on the 24$^{th}$ floor, in the boardroom of
the First Pennsylvania Banking and Trust Company, ready to pounce
on any news. Every half-hour, the press corps received word of an
exasperating delay in the tumultuous discussions eight floors below
them. After hours of waiting, a card game ensued among some of
the press in one corner of the room. A makeshift reporter-magician
practiced his craft for a few disinterested onlookers seated on the
floor in the opposite corner. All remained for hours upon hours with
eyes glancing at the hands of a large ticking clock on the wall above
them. They understood the judge had set a midnight deadline for all
documents to be signed, sealed and delivered.

By dinnertime, the media-men were bored and harried. By
the late evening, they were chugging coffee and raising exhausted
shoulders with arms extended palms up. By midnight, they were
catatonic for information and done in. Finally, they saw a glimpse
of Leonard Tose enter the room as the franchise's new owner, with
Jerry Wolman lagging behind alongside a collection of lawyers.

Just moments earlier, after close to fourteen hours of intense haggling, Wolman had transferred the Philadelphia Eagles to Tose in exchange for $16,155,000. The sum was a record amount for a professional sports organization. Tose spoke to all in the room, greeting the media in a gray jacket, gray shirt and gray-black-and-gold striped tie. He stated that he would fire Coach Kuharich and his entire staff, and also would be hiring a new General Manager. In the background, Jerry shrank inward in observable discomfort listening as his devoted staff of football brethren got the verbal sack.

Wolman hadn't slept since Tuesday, a span of nearly fifty hours. "It's hard to believe it is over," he said later with puffy eyes and an amputated soul.

The money from the sale of the team was divided among his creditors and stockholders. Wolman received none of it.

"What will you do now?" a reporter asked him at 1:00 a.m. as Jerry was leaving the building.

"Steal $3,000, go back to Shenandoah and retire," the former owner shrugged with an imperceptible smile. He then wished everyone well, flipped his Lucky Strike into the street and entered a car. The rags-to-riches-to-bankrupt visionary disappeared from sight into the dark early morning.

*****

"...In Philadelphia, he [Wolman] was like a chromed electric guitar in a window of 18ᵗʰ Century violins."

-Sandy Grady, The Evening Bulletin, May 2ⁿᵈ, 1969.

# "I'm Doing It For Me"

After a year's bankruptcy proceedings which followed the sale of the Eagles, and after having raised sufficient funds including a new plan of arrangement to provide his remaining creditors with a $3,000,000 note payable over a ten year period (which was fulfilled within three years), Jerry Wolman walked out of bankruptcy court in May of 1970 with no assets but for a wrinkled $35 savings bond. From the very beginning, he'd made the determination to save his many friends, partners, workmen and investors from the detriments he was now facing. He believed earnestly that his most important assets were people. In the end, because of Wolman's abiding credo, none of his creditors was hurt or hurting.

Jerry would continue his fight in courtrooms over the next several years regarding culpability over the construction of The John Hancock Center. He was eventually awarded $1,750,000 from a lawsuit against Tishman Construction Company, Skidmore, Owings and Merrill and Case Foundation, surrounding the Hancock Center's construction. Wolman gave half of the proceeds to his creditors in addition to paying off the $3,000,000 note. The majority of the other half was absorbed by legal fees.

Wolman's attorneys, within a month after the Eagles transaction, had also contacted Leonard Tose's counselors to demand the fulfillment set forth under the terms of their respective clients' repurchase agreement, to allow Wolman to buy back the Philadelphia Eagles from Tose. Tose refused to consummate the provisions, citing that Wolman's rights were to be honored by the new owner only if they were tied to the "Enterprises" plan of arrangement existing at the time the agreement had been signed. That plan had been later replaced. Wolman again battled in court for years over the wording of the agreement. He was defeated.

*****

Anne Wolman suffered a fatal heart attack on July 9th, 1971. She was just forty-one. Both her brother and mother had died of the same defective heart valve problem at the same exact age.

Her funeral, held at Tifereth Israel in Washington, D.C., was prolifically poignant and crowded with mourners. Thousands of telegrams, flowers and condolence-filled notes were sent with touching words to honor her memory. Over two thousand people attended Anne's memorial service. One could not see an end to the flow of cars in the procession. Rabbi Nathan Abramowitz, who'd befriended Jerry and Anne for nearly two decades, presided over the ceremony. Tearful eyes welled throughout the synagogue within moments of the start of the rabbi's most personal eulogy. He spoke from his heart about hers:

*"...Anne was a remarkable person: bright and cheerful, warm, friendly and outgoing. Her home was always open - but, even more important, she had an open heart. She loved her family in a very special way - but, beyond family, she loved people, everyone. She could sense a person's needs and hurts and could help. And she did so many hundreds of times. Some help publicly and with their resources. Anne helped privately and with herself..."*

Abramowitz continued, capturing Anne's magical essence with exceptional eloquence. Jerry listened in anguish, feeling lost and stunned. He was dazed and overcome during the tribute for his beloved wife and could barely part his lips during the service's prayers for the dead.

Over the next several days of sitting shiva with the Wolman family, the rabbi conducted each prayer of every service compassionately for them and for those paying their respects.

The following week, Jerry returned to the synagogue and knocked on the door of Rabbi Abramowitz's office. After a brief greeting, Wolman led the rabbi outside and showed him a lovely new Chevrolet station wagon parked adjacent to the synagogue's side entrance. Jerry reached into his pocket and started to hand Abramowitz a set of keys to the automobile he had purchased for the rabbi and his family.

"Jerry, I can't take this from you. This is beyond generous," the rabbi said incredulously to his vulnerable congregant.

"Please," Wolman responded, "take it."

Abramowitz shook his head "no" without speaking, but then thought best to question Jerry.

"How can you possibly be doing such a thing at a time like this? This is when you need to take care of yourself," cautioned Abramowitz. The rabbi then placed his hand on Jerry's shoulder and said, "I can't let you do this for me; I wouldn't feel right."

Jerry gazed at him a few seconds as if to gather energy. He lowered his head and subsequently looked back up at the rabbi compassionately.

"You don't understand," Jerry urged in a hoarse, humid voice. "I'm not doing this for you. I'm doing it for me."

Wolman quickly pushed the keys into Rabbi Abramowitz's motionless hands and told him, "This is what keeps me going."

*****

A few years later, after losing his home, Jerry moved into a modest apartment unit at Summit Hill, in the building complex that he had constructed himself a mere fifteen years before. Wolman was determined and ready to rebuild.

# "Jerry's Camelot"

"From the beginning he, and he alone, had been in control. Now, at the end, he and he alone has reaped the harvest of his whirlwind. We can't help Jerry Wolman but we can bleed with him, because we should. He tried to do something for Philadelphia which we despair of, and which others laugh at. He tried to give the city a distinction and a rationale for swaggering which had never even been dreamed of. He wanted the city to become an Athens-- an Athens in the Industrial East where such a beacon would have shown all the more brightly because of the decay surrounding it.

When he came to the City of Franklin Field, he was somehow associated with the tidal wave of optimism that ushered in the Kennedy years and that ended so dismally in 1964. He was connected in an invisible, intangible way with all that the Kennedy years of Camelot represented.

Philadelphia has been the butt of too many jokes, but still Wolman adopted the city. He made his fortunes a part of his welfare, and now, in an inextricable way for all those who feel and hurt just as deeply as Wolman, the future of Philadelphia hinges on the fate of this man.

The city may not find another Jerry Wolman. He wanted change to come and the first place he started was the uniquely urban drawing board of professional sports. If Philadelphia could win here, then there was hope in other areas.

When the bubble burst, the end lacked the painless swiftness which a man of Jerry Wolman's singular style and class merited. A

205

*slow, agonizing process consumed his energy and funds, but never his spirit.*

*His alternatives disappeared and his options were closed. All the troubles continued. Yet, on Christmas Eve, he could still buy every paper from every newsboy on Chestnut Street, and laugh and defend the mistakes that were rapidly destroying him--not because the mistakes were worth defending, but because Wolman had made the mistakes on his own, and to be Jerry Wolman means to take the good with the bad, alone.*

*This man's name should be heard whenever the Howard Hughes--J. Paul Getty--Hugh Hefner litany is recited. He deserves to be included--not simply because his actions were displayed on such a grand scale, or because he is a self-made man; but because he dreamed so gloriously and so sincerely.*

*A certain aspect of the fairy tale is gone. This makes the story more real, and the dollars and cents reality makes the pain more intense, the bitterness more long-lived, and the frustration more disconcerting...*

*Those who love football, and especially those who love the image which they envision Philadelphia as one day becoming, will never think of the Eagles without thinking of the owner, who loved them as most men love a woman...*

*Just as Robert Kennedy did, Wolman in his own way, dreamed dreams which we were too small to imagine. Now, at the end, when only the ideas remain, the least we can do is wish this very extraordinary man well."*

-Excerpt from award-winning journalist Mike Mallowe, following Wolman's final days in the "City of Brotherly Love" in May of 1969.

# Epilogue

*At present day, Jerry Wolman, remarkably spry, canters leisurely into the inner glow of a diner in Silver Spring, Maryland at 5:00 a.m., just as he had done the previous morning. After having built up a super-human tolerance to sleep deprivation over his almost eighty-three years, he sits alone at a vinyl booth in an otherwise empty eatery. Next to him, he has placed a large plastic bag containing his belongings. He removes a two-day-old folded Sunday newspaper from underneath his arm and spreads it fully open to the sports pages. The room is silent and still as he puts on his bifocals and adjusts his gaze across the section's headlines. Not a murmur can be heard in his mind of the cheers and accolades of the past. There is nothing, neither more nor less than his inconspicuous sense of serenity before the sunrise.*

*A waitress bumps through the swinging door leading from the kitchen, and having already heard the clapping and clicks of the front entrance opening and closing, she is carrying a ready glass of raspberry iced tea to place on his table.*

*"Hey there, you cute wonderful thing," he says zestfully to the young waitress with bags under her eyes. "How are you this morning?" he asks with interest.*

*Her face begins to beam in anticipation of his morning routine. She asks if he'd like the gluten-free pancakes. He stares at her dimples for a moment and grins.*

*"Boy oh boy," he replies shaking his head, "you're adorable. If I was only fifty years younger, we would definitely be together!"*

*The waitress blushes and giggles as always, and he affirms he'll indeed have the dietary pancakes. The smiling server never places a pen to her green order-pad.*

*"Thank you dear," he nods graciously as she saunters back into the kitchen. He sits, benign and unassuming. The "adorable" waitress never knows that at one time her charming elderly regular was a well-known icon in his day; in fact, one of the youngest, most successful, self-made men in the United States. And the thought has never occurred to him to tell her.*

*As he showers the Sweet'N Low into his glass, and droops his head to stir it, he can see his face's murky reflection off his drink. Thinking back to a time when his popularity and stature surpassed that of most city public figures, he reminisces and mumbles bitter-sweetly, "Money sure makes you more handsome, that's for certain; and a heck of a lot funnier too." But he quickly realizes that while perhaps time may have grayed and wrinkled his appearance, the years gone by have actually changed him very little. Through his much publicized meteoric rise and fall, he's still the same man he was before.*

*Perhaps it's the perceptions of others regarding him that may have changed. Nobody anymore asks for his autograph or business advice. His private planes had been permanently grounded and his prize-winning boats had drifted out to sea. His name no longer fills the sports pages beneath him and he hasn't built a tall building in a single bound for decades. He no longer belongs to country clubs, and his smiling celebrity caricatures no longer adorn any restaurant's walls. More importantly, he can no longer generously help people monetarily, and with easy bravado. He can, however, in the fifth quarter of his life, continue to spread as much thoughtfulness, humor and spirit to those around him as ever, bestowing gifts far more precious than his wealth. He has finally arrived at a personally placid place where kindheartedness and generosity are reflecting back upon him tenfold. And he wouldn't trade that grateful, welcomed feeling for the world.*

*Wolman is not your average "eighty-something." This morning his fingers ache with arthritis from having chatted online with his sixteen year-old granddaughter Andie. Communicating with her back and forth on the computer, which he maneuvers masterfully considering his age, Jerry playfully immerses himself into her life.*

*"It's important to interact with young people," he notes to himself, rubbing his sore hands above his napkin. "If you don't learn their lingo and what's going on, you might as well just grow old." Strangely, quite little about the man seated sprightly in his booth seems old. Perhaps it's his boundless energy or his intimacy with joy. And all that vigor and "joi de vivre" has been augmented by the close attention he pays to his seven grandchildren; all of whom have inherited fragmented pieces of his spirit.*

*Perusing through the Real Estate section of the weekend's paper, Wolman is taken back to days when he made five or six considerable deals a week. Visions of purchasing, planning and constructing buildings ramble like tumbleweed through his memory. Scanning the printed listings and data, he relives the tremendous sense of satisfaction each completed project brought. He immediately reflects on his oldest grandson Adam, a thirty-one-year-old builder in New York, who proudly carries his legacy in the field of endeavor that the elder Wolman helped shape. Just months before, Jerry had traveled to a suburb of New York City to view a finished home that his grandson had recently built. He stood outside in front of the house for nearly an hour.*

*As he turns the newspaper's pages to the Comics, he can't help but think of his grandson, Danny, who is now in his mid-twenties. Danny's sense of humor reminds the old notorious prankster so much of himself that Jerry lets escape a chuckle at the table. The two have always united in levity, bonding no matter the circumstances. Danny had once dislocated his knee at age seventeen. His grandfather was the first to arrive at the hospital and rush to his bedside.*

*"Grandpa, am I going to be okay?"*

*"Don't worry. This same injury happened to one of my friends growing up," Jerry comforted him.*

*The trembling teen asked with uncertainty, "Did he turn out alright?"*

*His grandfather hesitated, and then replied, "Actually, he died."*

*The boy's laughter could be heard three nursing stations away.*

\*\*\*\*\*

*By the time his pancakes arrive, the sun has risen and a few patrons have been seated in the diner. A bus driver is parked at one table, followed by a businessman who focuses on his cell phone at another. At 6:35 a.m., a group of young high school athletes wander in wearing their respective school-colored varsity team jackets. Upon noticing them, a nostalgic feeling spikes down his spine. The man who once stood atop the professional sports world as an NFL owner believes with absolute conviction that his happiest and most fulfilling experiences in and around sports came later on in life, simply watching his grandchildren play in school. Visions of his granddaughter Julie on the basketball court, or those of his grandson Brian on the football field, consume him with pride.*

*Brian was an exceptional wide-receiver in high school and his grandfather was his greatest supporter. Young Wolman held his school's record for touchdowns by a receiver and his grandfather still holds Brian's highlight reel tapes to prove it. Initially a walk-on at Hofstra University, he then earned a football scholarship, but not without a little lift from his grandfather. In the summer of 2004, during a hectic morning at work, the then seventy-seven-year-old received a frantic phone call from his grandson. His car had broken down in Delaware on his way to school. He was concerned he would be late for reporting to Hofstra's team's first summer workouts scheduled for that afternoon. Brian feared the consequences. The young receiver sweltered on the side of the road panicked about the state of his car, and more importantly, his football career. His grandfather raced without a trace of hesitation to meet him at the Chesapeake House exit in Delaware. Realizing that Brian's car needed considerable repair, and concurrently recognizing his grandson's consternation over football penalties, Jerry spontaneously drove his grandson to football camp himself, scurrying to be on time.*

*The unplanned, twelve-hour, roundtrip that had begun at mid-morning and ended late that night spanned no less than six hundred miles. But returning home was a breeze for the lone senior driver wheeling with the knowledge that his grandson had made it to college on a full ride.*

\*\*\*\*\*

*While searching for a straw at the diner's condiment station, one of the high school kids wearing a varsity jacket walks by Jerry.*

*"Excuse me," Wolman stops him. "What school do you play for?"*

*"Whitman," responds the jock awkwardly, pointing to the raised "W" machine-sewn on the left side of his jacket.*

*"My grandson played for Churchill," Jerry says proudly.*

*"We play them," challenges the boy.*

*Jerry leans in closer and cracks a big grandiose grin, "You're so lucky he's graduated."*

*In over a decade of his grandson's football career which had started in "Pee Wee" league and had successfully culminated in running routes over the lined fields at Hofstra, the old man never missed a game (with the exception of attending a funeral). No matter the distance in miles on his grandfather's odometer, Brian always saw him in the stands.*

*When Hofstra won the NCAA Atlantic-10 Conference Championship, Brian couldn't wait to show his grandfather the gold engraved championship ring. Proud beyond measure at his grandson's accomplishment, realizing the hard work, the commitment and dedication of the feat, the former professional football owner was moved to render a silent sob when Brian revealed it to him.*

*"I couldn't have done this without you," the young champion receiver said, and placed the ring in his grandfather's hand. Brian Wolman also understood the commitment and dedication made by his grandfather to him, and when the young man had reached the apex of his athletic career, he decided to share it with his biggest fan.*

*"Grandpa, I want you to have it; it's for you."*

*Jerry just stared at the shiny gold ring and measured its weight in his palm. It's more valuable to him than a Super Bowl trophy.*

\*\*\*\*\*

*Wolman's cell phone rings and startles him from his trance. "Hi Alan!" he answers excitedly. Now a successful financier at Credit Suisse Securities in New York City, his son calls while taking the ferry from New Jersey to get to work. Like two peas in a paternal pod, father and son roust each other as they make plans for the weekend. Nothing in their chemistry has changed since the days they'd shared football catches in front of fifty thousand Sunday fans at midfield before an NFL game. Though separated by a few states, one way or another they manage to find a way to get together on weekends. Jerry confirms all arrangements and hangs up the phone. Wolman treasures the togetherness of his family. He feels in his bones, still, the chill of the crushing misfortunes he and his children had once endured. And he's grateful for their strength.*

*He then opens the newspaper to the Style section and pampers his eyes reading through a number of cheerful couples' wedding announcements. Months prior in the fall, two of Wolman's granddaughters, Robyn and Julie, had been married weekends apart. Every crevice in his creased face had been soaked during both beautiful ceremonies. Having had everyone together for such wonderful, momentous occasions made him overjoyed. "That's what it's all about," he concludes, expounding tersely upon his sentiment of thankfulness; and he turns the page.*

*At 7:25 a.m., an elderly bald man in a blue sweater in the company of a woman on in her years sits a few tables away and notices Jerry. They shuffle their bodies closer together and begin whispering about him. After some elbow-prodding by his wife, the man inches over to Wolman's booth and clears his throat.*

*"You may not remember me," interrupts the man in the blue sweater, "but you really helped me out a long time ago."*

*"Of course I remember you, Buddy," a moniker Wolman only attributes to those he doesn't. "How are you?" he asks grinning.*

*"Things are better now. Bless you," says the bald gentleman, albeit in the absence of a sneeze. He continues, "Really, thank you. I'll always remember what you did."*

*Wolman pauses momentarily, and then warms to the conversant. "I'm glad to see you're well."*

*The man in the blue sweater nods his head respectfully at Jerry and then to his wife before withdrawing to his seat. Though cheered, Jerry sits scratching his head. "Gee, I wonder what the heck I did for him?"*

*Affable inquiries race through his head. Did he loan the man money? Did he get him a job or start him in business? Did he allow the man free rent in one of his apartment buildings? Did he pay the man's medical bills for him, his wife or his sick child? Maybe he gave the man a car or even built him a home. Or maybe the man was eating one night when he simply picked up his tab. Going back in his mind, he'd done so many of these types of things, and countless others for countless others; far too many to remember. Not a meal goes by that someone doesn't cordially engross him in the midst of his repast to thank him.*

\*\*\*\*\*

*The waitress touches his shoulder when she revisits him to ask if he's left room for dessert and coffee.*

*"Not this morning; but could you have them make a chicken Caesar salad and wrap it up to go?"*

*"Of course, not a problem," the waitperson rushes her words and heads to relay the message back to the kitchen.*

*"Thank you dear."*

*The chicken Caesar is for Bobbie Wolman, his wife of the last twenty-four years. Jerry fell in love with the most beautiful and equally kindhearted red-haired legal secretary from Chicago back in 1974. He asked that she move to Maryland, and though they didn't marry for eleven years thereafter, she was the best thing that could have happened to him. Bobbie devoted herself to Jerry and stood beside him through their lives' ups and downs, for better and for worse, through thick and thin. Fastening her safety-belt was sometimes necessary, as life can be quite a roller-coaster ride with the former tycoon. In the mid-70's, after having lost his legal battles to reclaim ownership of the Philadelphia Eagles, the varnished veteran builder made a successful comeback in real estate. He made $7,500,000 on a land and construction transaction. Then, through no fault of his own, the mortgage company that had handled all of* *his financing went into monetary purgatory right in the middle of his projects and wrecked them/him; a recurring nightmare.*

*He rebounded again in the mid-1980's with a smaller but lucrative deal, only to fall victim to a violent cash-wrenching crash on Wall Street. It would seem that all of the wind-at-his-back sails of luck that had blessed him in his twenties and thirties during thirteen windjammer years, had all but blown him away for good.*

*Many people wonder and speculate about his calamitous fall, and most are curious to know where he stands financially today. The plain answer is: it's really no one's business. He's just a gracefully aging man who lives within his means: somewhere in between blasphemous Chapter XI-debilitation and boldly being one of the world's richest men. If truth be told, he struggles mostly between his extraordinarily generous soul and his ordinary resources. Nonetheless, Wolman's abundant open-handed nature, notions and wisdom never take directions from his more modest circumstances and wherewithal. He still picks up the check for others in restaurants without fail, tips munificently and continues without hesitation to race to the aid of others, no matter what the personal cost.*

*Reflecting on his past, the former multi-millionaire expresses few regrets except when alluding to holding out for the eleven years' hiatus to marry his second wife. Otherwise, if he had to do it all over again, he'd theorize about his life and business in exactly the same way; sharing his fortune and success with others. That's not to say he is without scars. Losing the Philadelphia Eagles left him a hummingbird without a song. He cherished his beloved team and wanted it as a family treasure for generations, like the Rooney's in Pittsburgh, the Halas' in Chicago or the Mara's in New York.*

*Wolman holds little bitterness or contempt toward those who turned their backs on him in his time of need, exacerbating his fall. The smell of sulfur has left his nostrils. Those men to whom Wolman had given away so much, who profited during his own liquidity-strangulation are all quite wealthy today after having pounced upon the spoils of his imagination, dynamism and handiwork. Sadly, he quickly left Philadelphia in the middle of the night, without acknowledgement for any of the recognition he deserved.*

*In 2008, it was announced that the Spectrum in Philadelphia was* to be imploded and torn away. *The storied Spectrum arena had been home to professional championship teams in basketball and hockey, host to collegiate national championships, thousands of legendary game moments, historic events and concerts. The Spectrum was also the dramatic setting for the climactic fictional heavy-weight title fight in the film "Rocky." For twenty years, a statue of the famed Philly Italian Stallion had posed with its arms raised high, just outside its doors. The Spectrum defined the soul of the people and the city. It had been built from the heart and soul of Jerry Wolman. There has been great fanfare in the media over the demolition of such a sentimental landmark. An abundance of "grand farewell" events and ceremonies have transpired surrounding its demolition. But the man most responsible for the construction of the sports arena hasn't been invited to any of them. Wolman, whose downturn occurred at the time of the Spectrum's completion, never had the opportunity to watch a single game or event inside its doors.*

*****

*It's difficult not to think about "what ifs?" What if he hadn't hit a snag under the Hancock Center in Chicago? What if his creditors hadn't panicked and the real estate market hadn't collapsed? What if some of his partners hadn't backed out of a deal to save him? What if the court had not ruled against his assertion to later buy back the Philadelphia Eagles from Tose? What if he'd concentrated on saving and protecting his assets more than people?*

*His friend Ted Dailey once calculated a variety of salient figures and projections. They were based on Wolman's still owning the Philadelphia Eagles, the Flyers, the John Hancock Center, The Yellow Cab Companies, Connie Mack Stadium, The Spectrum and on completing the "City Within a City" project in Camden. To this Ted added all Jerry's countless apartment and office buildings that comprised his realty. Ted's estimate: Wolman's net worth would have been well over $10,000,000,000 today.*

*"If only I could have weathered the storms," he defends himself in the confines of the booth. Those billions would have made him one of the world's richest men.*

\*\*\*\*\*

*Jerry brings his wife Bobbie, employed as an administrative assistant for a church, her daily lunch. By the time the chicken Caesar salad arrives, he ruminates about Bobbie's coworkers.*

*"Excuse me, could you make that two more chicken Caesars? I'm sorry, Thank you dear."*

*As the patient young woman heads off again, Jerry wipes the syrup from his sticky fingers he had involuntarily dabbed while sliding his remaining silverware off to the table's side. He pulls out a large stack of envelopes along with some paper from his transparent bag of belongings. Attempting to keep them neat and organized, he meticulously positions the envelopes in front of him in columns. Tomorrow is his 83$^{rd}$ birthday. The day following his birthday holds special significance for him: It will be Valentine's Day as well as the 63$^{rd}$ wedding anniversary to his beloved first wife Anne. February 14th is always a powerful potion, and provides him an annual opportunity to let people know that he loves them.*

*Wolman removes from his cluttered bag a large bundle of letters and envelopes. The venerable man seemingly has an envelope for each year of his life. He writes with care to Lou Graboyes, an old friend in Philadelphia, and Claire Buete, his former secretary. He seals the envelopes addressed to Stanley Bobb, a former business partner now in Florida, and Leo Carlin, still in the Eagles ticket office after forty-five years. Then, he scribbles a playful loving note to his youngest ten-year-old grandson Michael.*

*An innumerable pile of letters, double-checked for spelling, has been laid fanning across the table. Their envelopes are addressed to males and females of all ages. Some of his coveted relationships span over six decades. Jerry works on a few unfinished letters painstakingly taking his time to inscribe varying quips, thoughts and feelings for each one. After the writing ceases, he seals the last envelopes and takes another sip of his iced tea, and sighs.*

*Wolman has spent what feels like three lifetimes working to stand high atop where he once had stood, churning to preserve all that he had created, and attempting to claw back to where he had been. Once described in the press as "indefatigable," he's finally getting tired of fighting to get his fortune back. There were so many near misses. But he never stopped trying. In his seventies, Wolman had organized and spearheaded a wealthy group of investors in an attempt to buy the Washington Redskins. But his 1998 bid wasn't selected. In the same manner, he also tried to repurchase the John Hancock Center at around that time, without triumph. He's spent countless hours working out ideas, concepts and ingenious business plans to hit just one more grand-slam of a deal so that he can once again "give" in the style to which he had once been accustomed.*

*His daughter Helene, a physical and spiritual replication of his late wife Anne, often reminds him that he is a success because of the person he is, not because of what he can provide for others. Helene is his touchstone and they meet for dinner so frequently it seems scheduled. Frustrated by her father's need to somehow make up for the past, she insists to him time and again that she is truly fortunate to have such an amazing one-of-a-kind father. Despite her comforting assurances, Jerry has never given up.*

*Wolman has lived one of the more intriguing and remarkable lives. He's rubbed elbows with gentlemen and gentlewomen named Kennedy, Sinatra, Ali and Lombardi. He pioneered the National Football League's marketing skills and championed the cause and creation of NFL Films. He brought a hockey franchise and a legendary arena to the city of Philadelphia and personally left an indelible mark on Philadelphia sports writers, players and fans. Though careening in memories of his family, his many friends and the way he lived his life, Jerry takes one final gulp of frosty tea with no ice remaining, and reveals philosophically and inwardly, "Maybe I am the world's richest man? Maybe my daughter's right, and perhaps Red Buttons' wife, the fortune-teller who had predicted I'd lose everything and one day get it all back, was right too."*

*Aside from his occasional intra-financial speed-bumps, he's encountered a fulfilling peacefulness. He's beloved, appreciated and respected. It is difficult if not impossible to perceive a man who has lived his life more richly; in legendary success and livid loss, enveloped in true love and hollowed by death's lingering, omnipresent heartache. His ambition to create happiness pulsates as his heart beats.*

*At 8:30 a.m., he sees the "to-go" bag and his check which had been placed silently on the table during his reverie. "Thank you dear," he concludes to himself softly.*

*He rakes in all of his belongings, carefully shoving them into his bag and yanks it over his forearm. He glances at the bill's thirty dollar total and leaves a crisp fifty edged under his plate. Upon departing with Bobbie's lunches and his valued Valentine's Day letters and cards for all, he traipses by the booth of the elderly woman and bald man in the blue sweater who had previously thanked him. He pauses and decides to delicately fish for information surrounding the circumstances in which he had helped the gentleman. "Who knows? Maybe he's well-off now and would like to repay me what I loaned him?" he jokes to himself.*

*What the man told Jerry caught him and his fishing rod off guard. In fact, Wolman had done nothing involving the man's purse strings. Decades ago the renowned tycoon/sports owner had learned that this man, a carpenter he'd met only once, had been taken seriously ill. Jerry simply took the time to obtain his hospital room number, called him and asked the man if there was anything he could do to help. The carpenter was surprised and thrilled by hearing the name of the caller. The tiny gesture seemed gargantuan to the bedridden workman and uplifted his sickly spirits. Jerry's ears reddened, tingling from the timeless testimony. Jerry Wolman felt like $10,000,000,000.*

*Walking out the door, Jerry skids into a scampering tiny tot girl wearing a mini-Philadelphia Eagles jersey. Her mother is about to scold her.*

*"Hey there Cutie," Wolman says. "Are you an Eagles fan?"*

*"Yes," says the little girl at Jerry's welcome intervention.*

*"Why aren't you a Redskins fan?" he asks the child in the D.C. area diner, now holding her mother's hand.*

*"Because my parents are from Pennsylvania, and my Daddy loves the Eagles," she answers adorably.*

*Wolman grins warmly at the little girl and kneels down as if about to draw up a play in a huddle. "Little lady, if that's true, then you'll never guess what I'm about to tell you..."*

*"What?" she innocently replies, leaning closer with naive interest.*

*He proudly brushes the little angel's nose with the tip of his index finger and boasts, "Tell your father I'm from Shenandoah!"*

*Jerry displays a syrupy smile to the little girl's mother and tiptoes out of the diner contently.*

# References

Bilovsky, Frank. 1966. *"Wolman Seeks to Bring Big League Hockey Here...
Jerry Plans New Arena, Bids for NHL Franchise"* – Philadelphia Bulletin.
February 10.

Brady, Dave. 1967. *"Wolman Defends Eagles' Solvency"* – The Washington Post.
November 15.

Brady, Frank. 1969. *"Longest Day for Press"* – The Evening Bulletin. February 5.

*"Business in Deep Water."* 1967. Time. November 24.

*"Chicago Skyline Adds a New Dimension."* 1966. Business Weekly. February 4.

Dell, John. 1964. *"Rozelle Cuts Ribbon To Open Eagle Office."* The Philadelphia
Inquirer.

Dell, John. 1964. *"Wolman Gets Into Brawl After Game"* – The Philadelphia
Inquirer. July 8.

*"Eagles Offer Mack Stadium To Philadelphia for 50 Cents."* 1964. New York
Times. June 4.

*"Eagles' Owner in Financial Straits."* 1967. New York Times. November 15.

Forbes, Gordon. 1964. *"Site Brings $757,500 in 10-Min. Sale."* Philadelphia
Inquirer. June 23.

*"Friends Raise $Million, But Jerry Turns It Down." 1968.* The Philadelphia Daily
News. January 12.

Grady, Sandy. 1967. *"Generosity Is Wolman's Problem."* The Evening Bulletin.
October 23.

Grady, Sandy. 1969. *"The Party is Over For Jerry Wolman."* The Evening
Bulletin. May 2.

Grady, Sandy. 1969. *"Tose Wishes Wolman Well."* The Evening Bulletin. January 26.

Jewell, David A. 1967. *"Rockville Bank Is Suing Wolman for $236,000."* The
Washington Post. December 5.

Jewell, David A. 1967. *"Wolman Reveals $15.5 Million Loss."* Washington Post.
November 15.

Lau, Emily. Modern Marvels. 2005. *"The John Hancock Center."* The History
Channel. June 8.

221

Mallowe, Mike. 1969. *"Jerry's Camelot, Wolman: Bearing the Butt of the Philadelphia Joke."* The Evening Bulletin. May 3.

Mallowe, Mike. 1988. *"Forty Over Eighty."* Philadelphia Magazine. September.

Morrison, John F. 1969. *"Tose Gets Eagles' Control, Heeds "Joe Must Go" Critics."* The Evening Bulletin. May 2.

Padwe, Sandy. 1967. *"Wolman's Day Ends Dismally."* The Philadelphia Inquirer. October 23.

Shecter, Leonard. 1964. *"Owner."* New York Post. December 20.

Shefski, Bill. 1967. *"The Insolvent Santa."* Philadelphia Daily News. December 27.

Staff Reporter. 1966. *"Eagles' Ed Snider Adopted as "Son" by Mahanoy City Citizens."* Shenandoah Evening Herald. May 23.

Staff Reporter. 1967. *"Jerry Wolman Files For Bankruptcy Under Chapter 11 Provisions."* Wall Street Journal. December 14.

Weir, Frank H. 1966. *"Nobody Makes It By Himself."* The Philadelphia Inquirer Magazine. April 24.

Willmann, John B. 1967. *"Washington Realtors Rooting for Wolman."* Washington Post. November 16.

Willmann, John B. 1965. *"It's a Nice Place to Stop for That 2nd Cup."* The Washington Post. October 2.

Willmann, John B. 1963. *"Now He's a $50-Million-a-Year Builder."* The Washington Post. February 9.

"Wolman Sells Hockey Stock." 1967. The Baltimore Sun. August 27.

Ziff, Sid. 1964. *"Dropout to Riches."* Los Angeles Times. November 6.